General editor: Graham Handley

Brodie's Notes on Charlotte Brontë's

Villette

Graham Handley MA PhD
Formerly Principal Lecturer in English, College of All Saints, Tottenham

Pan Books London, Sydney and Auckland

First published 1988 by Pan Books Ltd,
Cavaye Place, London SW10 9PG
9 8 7 6 5 4 3 2 1
© Pan Books Ltd 1988
ISBN 0 330 50274 3
Photoset by Parker Typesetting Service, Leicester
Printed and bound in Great Britain by
Richard Clay Ltd, Bungay, Suffolk

Contents

Page references are to the Penguin Classics edition of *Villette*, but as references are also given to particular chapters, the Notes may be used with any edition of the book.

Preface

The **intention** throughout this study aid is to stimulate and guide, to encourage the reader's *involvement* in the text, to develop disciplined critical responses and a sure understanding of the main details in the chosen text.

Brodie's Notes provide a summary of the plot of the play or novel followed by act, scene or chapter summaries, each of which will have an accompanying critical commentary designed to underline the most important literary and factual details. Textual notes will be explanatory or critical (sometimes both), defining what is difficult or obscure on the one hand, or stressing points of character, style or plot on the other. Revision questions will be set on each act or group of chapters to test the student's careful application to the text of the prescribed book.

The second section of each of these study aids will consist of a critical examination of the author's art. This will cover such major elements as characterization, style, structure, setting, theme(s) or any other aspect of the book which the editor considers needs close study. The paramount aim is to send the student back to the text. Each study aid will include a series of general questions which require a detailed knowledge of the set book; the first of these questions will have notes by the editor of what *might* be included in a written answer. A short list of books considered useful as background reading for the student will be provided at the end.

Graham Handley

The author and her work

Charlotte Brontë was born on 21st April 1816 at Thornton in Bradford, where her father Patrick, who was of Irish extraction, was Rector. Her mother, who came from a Methodist family in Penzance, Cornwall, had met her future husband when she was staying in Leeds. Maria Branwell brought her husband an annuity of £50 when they were married in 1812. Charlotte was the couple's third child, Maria and Elizabeth being babies of one and two years' old respectively when she was born. A brother, Patrick Branwell (but always known by the latter name) and two more sisters, Emily and Anne, were to arrive in the next few years, Anne, the youngest, being born at the beginning of 1820.

Soon after Anne's birth, Mr Brontë and his family moved to Haworth near Keighley in Yorkshire, where he had just been appointed parson. When Mrs Gaskell came to write her celebrated *Life of Charlotte Brontë* (1857), one of the classic biographies which is still in print, she provided many facts and incidents which define the bleakness of the country around Haworth. She described the people who lived in the area as rough but 'powerful in mind and body'. The parsonage where the Brontë's lived was quite small, and both parsonage and church were below the level of the churchyard which lay on two sides of the garden. The situation was both depressing and unhealthy. It was subjected to the fierce winds and driving rain which were characteristic of the district, and exposure to them certainly helped to sow the seeds of illness in the Brontë children. Nevertheless from an early age they chose to walk on the moors that rose above the village and which, as time went on, they grew to love passionately.

In 1821 Mrs Brontë died and the children, who were already 'grave and silent beyond their years', were thrown more and more upon their own devices. Their aunt Miss Branwell came from Penzance to look after them; she was a kind woman who was determined to do her duty by this motherless family, but she found the change from the relatively warm south to the cold and bleak north distasteful, and spent much of her time in her bedroom. Though the children respected her they seem to have had little warm affection for her. She taught the girls needle-work and household management, at which Charlotte was to excel. Meanwhile, the Reverend Patrick Brontë was responsible for his children's lessons. He was an eccentric man, took his meals alone because of digestive trouble, and his theories of education were prompted by a 'desire to make his children hardy and indifferent to the pleasures of eating and of dress'. His decision to send his elder daughters Maria and Elizabeth to Cowan Bridge school in 1824 had momentous results for Charlotte's later fictional career. As Mrs Gaskell, invited by Mr Brontë to write a biography of Charlotte, wrote:

Miss Brontë more than once said to me that she would not have written what she did of Lowood in *Jane Eyre* if she had thought the place would have been so immediately identified with Cowan Bridge, although there was not a word in her account of the institution but what was true at the time when she knew it.

Maria was far superior to any of her play-fellows and companions, and yet, she had faults so annoying that she was in constant disgrace with her teachers and an object of merciless dislike to one of them, who is depicted as 'Miss Scatcherd' in *Jane Eyre*. I need hardly say that Helen Burns is as exact a transcript of Maria Brontë as Charlotte's wonderful power of reproducing character could give.

Life of Charlotte Brontë (1857)

After the deaths of Maria and Elizabeth in 1825, and the removal of Charlotte and Emily from the school, the children were increasingly driven into the world of their imagination. They built their own land of make-believe, putting their fancies into words, their juvenilia existing today in a number of tiny books about two inches square in which their stories were written. The handwriting is so minute that it can hardly be read without a magnifying glass. In her *History of the Year 1829* Charlotte tells us how their plays originated:

I will sketch the origin of our plays more explicitly if I can. First *Young Men*. Papa brought Branwell some wooden soldiers at Leeds; when Papa came home it was night and we were in bed, so next morning Branwell came to our door with a box of soldiers. Emily and I jumped out of bed, and I snatched up one and exclaimed. 'This is the Duke of Wellington! This shall be the Duke!' When I had said this, Emily likewise took up one and said it should be hers; when Anne came down she said one would be hers.

Branwell describes how the twelve wooden soldiers (now become twelve young men) founded a kindgom in Africa called Great

Glass Town, about which innumerable histories, newspapers, magazines were written by the children. When Charlotte went away to school in 1831, the four 'chief genii' who helped the twelve, Talli (Charlotte), Brannii (Branwell), Emmii (Emily), and Annii (Anne) decided to destroy the Great Glass Town. Charlotte wrote a poem about this, but while she was away Emily and Anne invented another world of make-believe, this time called Gondal. When Charlotte returned, she and Branwell originated yet another kingdom, this one being given the name of Angria, which lay in the East of Glass Town and was conquered by two pitiless Dukes. Charlotte found this dream world a pleasant escape from the tedium of reality, but she was aware of the dangers of living too much in the imagination – 'it makes the dreamer feel society, as it is, wretchedly insipid' – and in 1839 she renounced the land of Angria.

Charlotte stayed at Roe Head school for eighteen months, 'a plain, short-sighted, oddly-dressed, studious little girl', becoming friends with Ellen Nussey and Mary Taylor. The letters and descriptions of these two provided Mrs Gaskell with much material about Charlotte when she came to write her biography of the novelist. On her return home Charlotte helped to educate her younger sisters until, in 1835, she returned to Roe Head as a teacher, taking Emily with her. Later on Emily became so homesick that she had to go back to Haworth, and the same thing happened to Anne, who had replaced her.

Charlotte and Anne later obtained posts in private families, but both were unfortunate in their employers, and soon changed their positions. Meanwhile Branwell, who had hoped to study painting at the Royal Academy School, was disappointed – he had obviously yielded to some degree of dissipation – and tried job after job in turn, losing each one. Charlotte wanted them all to open a school, but the competition was such that she decided that it was best if she studied in Brussels for some time in order to equip herself better for this scheme. It was in 1842 that she and Emily became pupils at the *pensionnat* of Madame Héger. They worked hard there, but decided to return home when they learned that their Aunt Branwell had died. Emily elected to remain with her father while Charlotte returned once more to Brussels, this time in the capacity of pupil-teacher. Her Brussels life is to some degree mirrored in *Villette* (with some fascinating insights into it too in *The Professor*), and it is apparent that she experienced much loneliness and depression. This was in part traceable to homesickness, for the holidays were a particularly difficult period for her to get through, but in part also to the fact that she had fallen in love with Madame's husband, Monsieur Héger, who was a professor at the boys' school next door. Charlotte returned home in 1844, and plans for their own school were again in the forefront of the sisters' minds.

But this time a domestic crisis shattered their hopes. Branwell came home in disgrace, and from that time until his death three years later he was the cause of constant concern to his family. Charlotte's courage and integrity made her push on for herself and her sisters, and all three decided to try to publish their poems. The girls had to pay ten guineas each to see *Poems by Currer, Ellis and Acton Bell* (1846) get into print, and another £13 to advertise it. The collection made little or no impact, but it gave the sisters the spur to try to get their novels published.

In 1847 Emily's *Wuthering Heights* and Anne's *Agnes Grey* were accepted for publication, but Charlotte's *The Professor* was rejected. It is a great tribute to her stamina and application that she still set to work on *Jane Eyre* despite the fact that her father had just had an operation for the removal of cataracts. When *Jane Eyre* was published it met with high praise from such discerning critics as Thackeray and Leigh Hunt, but *Wuthering Heights, Agnes Grey* and *The Tenant of Wildfell Hall* did not at first attract critical approval. Many people assumed that the novels were written by the same person using different names. There was some suspicion of double-dealing, and accordingly Anne and Charlotte went to the offices of their publisher in London and convinced him of their integrity. Meanwhile, unremitting family sorrow was near at hand. Branwell died on 24 September 1848, and a few weeks later Emily died too. Anne was already weakening. She died in May 1849 with Charlotte in attendance on her.

Charlotte felt keenly the loss of her two beloved sisters, but she returned to the writing of her next novel, *Shirley*. There was no one to talk to, no one to confide in, but she pressed on with this important novel. It is set in the latter part of the Napoleonic War and deals with the Luddite riots over machine-breaking. Central to it is the woman theme, which is virtually present in all of Charlotte's books, and which determinedly asserts the need for a positive occupation for women. *Shirley* was well received, and soon Charlotte began to pay the first of a series of visits to London. She met Thackeray, to whom she dedicated the second edition of *Jane Eyre* (without perhaps realizing that Thackeray, like Rochester, had a mad wife who had once tried to commit suicide). Charlotte also became acquainted with her future biographer, Mrs Gaskell, herself a successful social novelist and the author of the superbly ironic and much-loved *Cranford*.

Charlotte's life at Haworth became more lonely and dreary. She thought she heard her sisters' voices and their cries, in much the same way as Jane hears Rochester's voice calling her name in the novel. The writing of *Villette* followed and is dealt with below, but her private life now took on another degree of suffering and intensity. It seems likely that over the years several suitors were interested in Charlotte, but in 1852 her father's curate Arthur Bell Nicholls nerved himself to propose to her. Not only did she reject him (but with kindness) she also had to endure her father's vindictive attitude towards Mr Nicholls. When he returned to a neighbourhood parish in 1854, however, she decided to accept him and her father was won over to consent. Her happy marriage lasted only a few months. On 31st March 1855 Charlotte died, while her father lived on until 1861. Before that he had asked Mrs Gaskell to undertake the biography of his talented daughter. This she did, and the *Life of Charlotte Brontë* was published in 1857. It ends with a fitting tribute from Charlotte's friend Mary Taylor. Her words, I think, sum up the life and concerns of a great writer, and stand there as a mark of serious intention and rather sad commentary:

She thought much of her duty, and had loftier and clearer notions of it than most people and held fast to them with more success ... All her life was but labour and pain; and she never threw down the burden for the sake of present pleasure.

Writing and publication

Villette is a fictional representation of Charlotte's experiences in Brussels, with Paul Emanuel approximating to Monsieur Héger (whom Charlotte loved) and Madame Beck to his wife. Other biographical identifications include Charlotte's publisher George Smith and his mother as Graham and Mrs Bretton. Charlotte's biographer Winifred Gérin believes that Paulina is based upon Mr Gaskell's youngest daughter Julia.

Villette was written under conditions of loneliness and oppression. This accounts for it being such a sombre book. By middle to late 1851 Charlotte was at work on the novel, but Mr Brontë became ill in October and Charlotte had to adandon her work. She became increasingly depressed herself, something she experienced, quite naturally, at intervals since the deaths of her sisters and Branwell in 1848 and 1849. In a letter to Mrs Gaskell she recorded her tendency towards illness and depression in the latter part of each year. In another letter she defines her state of mind, and we notice how close it is to Lucy Snowe's reactions in the novel:

Some long stormy days and nights there were when I felt such a craving for support and companionship as I cannot express. Sleepless I lay awake night after night . . . (12 April 1852).

Her only comfort, apparently, was her friendship with George Smith, though even here she was capable of passionately misjudging him. She turned down an offer to go and see him at Christmas (1851), and during this time she was so incapacitated that she could do very little writing. She suffered from jaundice, and was further debilitated by the death of Emily's favourite dog Keeper at the beginning of December. She could not see her way forward in life at this time. She feared that she herself was suffering from the lung trouble which had killed her sisters, and George Smith believed that her health had been so seriously undermined that she would not live to complete her novel. But her motivation, as always, was strong, and she wrote to Mrs Smith in January 1852 that her visit to London would be undertaken when she delivered the completed manuscript of her book. Throughout the spring and summer of 1852 she was still unable to write: her father suffered a slight stroke, while her friend James Taylor caused her further stress by ceasing to write to her from India. With typical dedication and assertion of will she resumed work on *Villette* in August, and in a sustained spell of discipline and imagination she succeeded in completing it by 20 November 1852. George Smith was moved to criticize the excessive morbidity (as it seemed to him) of Lucy Snowe, but Charlotte defended this in no uncertain terms, since her experiences were Lucy's and they had really happened. As Winifred Gérin puts it:

What emerges with inescapable clarity is that, as the course of her own destiny unfolded in the decisive year 1852, both the memory and the lesson of her greatest experience in life – her love for Monsieur Héger – returned with new meaning and emphasis and took possession of her mind. *Villette* is the last great *devoir* Mlle Charlotte accomplished at the instigation of her Master.

Charlotte Brontë (1967)

And Charlotte's great contemporary, Anthony Trollope, remarked discerningly 'She must herself have been in love with some Paul when she wrote the book, and have been determined to prove to herself that she was capable of loving someone whose exterior circumstances were mean and in every way unprepossessing.' (*An Autobiography*, 1883).

Charlotte rejected romance in her novel just as she had been forced to reject romantic reality in life. But that reality is transferred to her fiction with indelible force. Even her father had expressed the wish for a happy ending to *Villette*, but Charlotte was as inexorable as ever. The effect of the novel on many readers is perhaps best summed up by Marian Evans when she says, in a letter to her friend Mrs Caroline Bray, 'I have been reading *Villette*, a still more wonderful book than *Jane Eyre*. There is something almost preternatural in its power.' A few years after this statement Marian Evans was to achieve immortality as George Eliot. It is a tribute to her critical powers that thus early she was so transcendently aware of Charlotte Brontë's unique qualities.

With the novel in her publisher's hands, Charlotte was distressed by the fact that George Smith only offered to pay her £500 for it (the same sum that she had received for *Jane Eyre* and *Shirley*). She was also pressurized by him to alter and modify certain emphases in the final volume, but she refused to compromise either her principles of truth or her artistic faith. She insisted on retaining the essential ambiguity of the ending. She compelled George Smith to refuse permission for a French translation, though a pirated edition of the novel appeared in French in 1855. The English edition was published at the end of January 1853 to almost universal critical acclaim. Harriet Martineau, Charlotte's friend, provoked her wrath however by her castigation of the love situations, while Thackeray privately admitted his dislike of these elements. *Villette* remains in all its intensity and integrity a great novel, its force for truth and its enigmatic elements perhaps somewhat too strong for the period in which it was written. Posterity, however, has no doubt of its signal qualities.

Plot

Lucy Snowe goes to stay with her godmother Mrs Bretton at Bretton (in Yorkshire). Soon she learns that a visitor is expected, and the small Paulina Mary Home, whose mother has died, arrives. The child tries hard to be independent, and focuses her love on Graham Bretton, Mrs Bretton's sixteen-year-old son. At this stage Lucy is observer and reporter of what goes on.

For the next eight years Lucy is companion to a crippled lady, Miss Marchmont. When the latter dies Lucy goes to London, and from there to the French port of Boue-Marine hoping to obtain employment abroad. On board she meets Ginevra Fanshawe, a spoilt and snobbish girl who is a pupil at Madame Beck's school in Villette (Brussels). Lucy learns from her that an English governess is required. Madame Beck takes her in, and employs her as governess to her children.

Lucy learns French and soon obtains a teaching position after Madame has removed one of her staff. Madame is a good organizer and runs the school well, but she spies (certainly on Lucy) and employs others to spy for her. This is the secret of her power.

Ginevra confides in Lucy about her two loves. Then Dr John is called in to treat one of Madame Beck's children who has broken an arm. Lucy at once sees that this is the Englishman who helped her when she first arrived at Villette. He is also Ginevra's suitor, the other being the effeminate aristocratic puppy, de Hamal. Lucy also agrees to perform in the school play, and comes under the positive direction and influence of M.Paul.

During the summer holidays Lucy remains at the school, alone except for a cretin whom she looks after. She passes through a crisis, what seems to be a mental breakdown and, despite her rigid anti-Catholicism, goes to the confessional at a Catholic church in her desperation. The priest, later identified as Père Silas, realizes she is ill. She collapses but is cared for by Dr John, who takes her to his home.

As she recovers she realizes that Dr John is the grown-up Graham Bretton, and she is being cared for by his mother. Dr John is still infatuated by Ginevra, but one night at the theatre with Lucy and his mother he sees that Ginevra is mocking Mrs Bretton, and his insight into the real nature of Ginevra begins. After her recovery Lucy returns to the pensionnat, her feelings for Dr John having deepened. She receives her first kind letter from him, reads it, and then becomes somewhat hysterical when she sees an apparition – that of the nun who is supposed to haunt the place. Dr John is soon there to comfort her, and retrieves her letter, which she thinks in her panic she has lost. One night they go to the theatre. There is a fire and Dr John and Lucy help a man and his daughter. Later we learn that they are M.de Bassompierre and his daughter Paulina Mary, who had stayed at Bretton all those years ago.

Soon Lucy realizes that Madame Beck has been going through her letters. She decides to hide them, then sees the mysterious nun again. M.Paul is critical of her, but she is attracted to him despite his mercurial, unpredictable temperament. As their relationship deepens Lucy is despatched by Madame Beck to see an old deformed lady, Madame Walravens. M.Paul was engaged to her granddaughter, but the latter died in a convent. Lucy later tells M.Paul that she knows his secret. They agree to be friends.

Meanwhile the courtship of Paulina and Dr John continues. M.de Bassompierre is against the match, but finally gives in, Lucy having made it clear that she is on the side of the young lovers. Suddenly comes the news that M.Paul is to go to the West Indies to look after the financial interests of Madame Walravens there. Lucy is upset, but gets a letter from M.Paul saying that she must be ready to receive him. She is given an opiate by Madame Beck after she has waited for a long time to see M.Paul, but it does not take effect, and Lucy becomes suddenly wakeful. She goes to the main park in Villette where she observes the Brettons and the Bassompierres and then M.Paul, Madame Beck and their 'junta', including M.Paul's goddaughter and Père Silas. She goes back to the pensionnat and finds the clothes of the 'nun' on the bed. A note from Ginevra tells her that de Hamal has used the disguise to see her, Ginevra. She has now eloped with him.

M.Paul finally comes to Lucy, gets rid of Madame Beck and takes Lucy to some apartments which he has purchased for her as a school. They express their love for each other, and then he leaves. She runs the school successfully, and he writes to her regularly. The story ends ambiguously. M.Paul is due to return, but there are reports of terrible storms. Does he survive them? Are they in Lucy's imagination or the cause of his death? We are left with the impression that whichever it is their love is inviolable.

Chapter summaries, critical commentaries, textual notes and revision questions

Volume One
Chapter 1
Bretton

The first-person narrator describes her visits to her godmother, Mrs Bretton and her son, Graham. Lucy Snowe, the narrator, tells of one visit in the autumn when she finds that a little girl is expected to stay there, her godmother giving her briefly the circumstances which occasion the visit. The child proves to be a very positive little character, but Lucy, who sleeps in the same room with her, notices that she weeps quietly before she goes to sleep. The next morning she finds the child Polly (really Paulina Mary) up and washing herself. Mrs Bretton is concerned about her, but wisely asserts that if she takes a fancy to someone in the house she will become secure.

Commentary

For readers of *Jane Eyre* the supposedly autobiographical narrative will be familiar. We note the simplicity of the style, the comfort that Lucy derives from her visits, the natural and easy description which is the hallmark of the story-teller – we want to read on. There is a pleasant and nostalgic feel to the writing. The account of Mrs Bretton is sympathetic. Lucy, like Jane before her, enters into monologues with herself. It is a mark of her character. The brief retrospect on the Home marriage explains much, but the coming arrival of the child arouses narrative expectation. The child herself is a mixture of precocity and vulnerability, her independence and imitation of grown-up mannerisms and speech scarcely concealing her suffering at being separated from her father. Her pride only allows her to weep quietly so as not to draw attention to herself. At this stage Lucy is merely observer and narrator. Almost the whole of the narrative focus is on the child. Paulina (as we shall come to know her) has a remarkable degree of outward self-possession, and we feel for her and with her. She is also bossy and somewhat objectionable, as we see in her resistance to Lucy. The chapter ends on a note of genuine pathos with Paulina unable to eat.

brunette Dark-skinned.
Christian and Hopeful ... 'green trees on each bank ...' The first the main character, the second his friend, in John Bunyan's celebrated Christian allegory *The Pilgrim's Progress* (1678).
'Of what are these things signs and tokens?' Lucy frequently talks to herself, sometimes personifying her thoughts and emotions. In a way it underlines her lonely and withdrawn nature.
subjoined Added.
savant Man of learning (French).
wrote *de* before his name i.e. belonging to, descended from, an aristocratic family.
'Harriet, I must be put to bed,' This is typical of Paulina's little-grown-up behaviour.
against the time When.

Chapter 2
Paulina

The effect of the child's moping is described, with Lucy feeling sometimes that Paulina is so unearthly that the room is haunted rather than filled by her tiny presence. With the arrival of her father all this changes, and Paulina's complete devotion to him is evident. Lucy feels that these attentions are too much and that the child is a busybody. Her second focus of interest comes with the arrival of Graham Bretton. He is described by Lucy as a spoiled boy and makes much of the fact that he has not been introduced to Paulina. This is soon remedied, and there is a kind of communication between the two. Graham, however, annoys his little visitor by picking her up and holding her above his head. She feels keenly the loss of dignity.

Commentary

The effect of Paulina's behaviour is very marked upon Lucy herself, but there is some irony here, since Lucy says that 'I, Lucy Snowe, plead guiltless of that curse, an overheated and discursive imagination' (page 69) a remark which we may accept at this stage but which is certainly untrue of the later Lucy, who is a prey to various morbid fears and has nothing if not a vivid imagination. There is also something condemnatory in Lucy's attitude towards Paulina's prayers and depressive tendencies, and a patronizing tone is adopted towards Paulina's sensitivity. All this is ironic in view of Lucy's own later suffering. Finely economical imagery is used to convey Paulina's relationship to and dependence on her father – 'her mind had been filled from his, as the cup from the flagon.' (page 71). The child's devotion to her father – his seeming obliviousness at times – is movingly and pathetically conveyed. Lucy's initial description of Graham is also ironic, but there is much humour in the description of the whimsical and idiosyncratic interaction between him and Polly. Both ape polite manners, Graham satirically and Paulina with a kind of precocious self-importance which is at once endearing and ridiculous. At one stage he calls her 'Miss Home' and tells her that he is her slave – a subtle look forward, since this is what he is to become much later in the action. The dialogue between them is convincing within the context. Graham reveals a kind of insensitivity in picking her up so freely, and Paulina an injured pride in reacting as she does.

antipodes i.e. at the opposite ends.
I, Lucy Snowe ... Lucy commonly refers to herself. Here she is quick to qualify what she feels, but this is an indication of her sensitivity – she is afraid of her own morbid imagination, which later overcomes her on occasions.
Like a bird ... or any other swift thing Note the economy of the simile – *Villette* is laced with such sudden and vivid expressions.
rapt i.e. gathered up, enclosed.
nonpareil Unequalled.
queer ... queerer i.e. odd, different (without any of the modern associations with the word).

Chapter 3
The Playmates

Paulina ostentatiously makes a keepsake handkerchief for her father. Graham continues to tease her, but a rapport, an understanding is built up between them, particularly after Graham affects to be injured by her. Her parting from her father reduces her to tears. Graham now begins to take an interest in her, and she responds by helping to get his breakfast, even imitating his mother's manner in her treatment of him. His interests at school become her interests, but there is hurt for

Paulina when Graham thoughtlessly rejects her from his birthday celebrations with his friends. She sulks with him, but afterwards they make it up and she learns much from him. She
confesses to him that she loves him. Later she shows Lucy a book
Graham has given her, but is angry with Lucy when she raises
the question of her father. She is very upset when she has to go,
though Lucy takes her to say goodbye to Graham.

Commentary

The focus on Paulina continues, with her devotion to her father
being succeeded by a like devotion to Graham. She is so vulnerable as she shows in her reaction to Graham's offer of the
etching and the purchase price of a kiss. The picture of Graham
himself is that of a typical boy – he finds Polly a pleasant form of
diversion, more attractive than either his mother or Lucy as a
companion for his high spirits. The business of Graham's
injured eye is rather heavy-handed comedy, though the situation between himself and Paulina is a natural one. One of Charlotte's great strengths is her ability to convey the spirit and
exchanges of an interior like this. At the parting with her father
it is Polly who shows the greater self-possession. Lucy boasts
here of her own calmness in the situation, and we feel that her
complacency is misguided in view of her own intensely emotional nature which she resists for so long. Polly has a deep need
to be loved (so does Lucy), hence her transference of feeling to
Graham. Lucy rather resents these officious manifestations, as
she chooses to think them. Polly further shows her capacity for
adaptation in her thoroughgoing absorption in Graham's life
and interests. Lucy is somewhat critical of this, and we again see
Polly's vulnerability when Graham rejects her and she tries –
unsuccessfully – to keep him at a distance thereafter. Lucy
however is quick to recognize Polly's capacity to learn and her
dramatic flair. Lucy herself is aware of Polly's fixation on Graham, and tries to break the news that she has to go to her father
gently by asking her if she would like to travel. This follows
Polly's delight in her book and her loving associations of Graham with it. Graham's matter-of-fact acceptance of the news that
'Little Mousie' is going contrasts with the child's intensity of
passion for him. We warm somewhat to Lucy as her concern for
Polly increases, and her taking Polly to say goodnight to Graham

shows how far her own heart has moved. Lucy tries to impart her wisdom to the child about the difference in her age and Graham's. It is a measure of the quality of Charlotte Brontë's writing that we are ourselves moved by Polly's departure, which hardly touches Graham.

'Why hast thou forsaken me?' A deliberate echo of the words of Christ on the Cross.

I, Lucy Snowe, was calm. This is one of the statements which put us out of sympathy with Lucy in the early stages of the novel. As her character unfolds, however, we see that the calmness is imposed and that she is of a very emotional temperament.

tête-à-tête Together, intimately.

'I'm as weak as a rush.' Note the affectation of Graham here (and the effective brevity of the image).

the game of romps i.e. playing about, picking up Paulina.

the Grand Turk i.e. the ruler of the Ottoman (Turkish) empire.

by inculcating some of those maxims . . . ready for application Lucy is pompous, pedantic and unsympathetic here – she becomes much more human later. We get the impression that she is a little jealous of the attention that Polly gets.

a changeling A child substituted for another child, or an elf-child left by the fairies.

Joseph cast into the pit; the calling of Samuel; Daniel in the lion's den For the first see Genesis 37:23–4, for the second I Samuel 3:1–18, for the third Daniel 6:10–24.

Odalisque Female slave, concubine in Sultan's harem.

Kim – kim – borazo Chimborazo, mountain in Ecuador, South America.

Chapter 4
Miss Marchmont

Eight years pass for Lucy, she never returns to Bretton, and we are left with the impression that she has had a rough period of time to live through. She is thrust upon her own devices, and goes to work for a crippled lady in her neighbourhood, Miss Marchmont. At first she has her doubts about what she is taking on. But she respects Miss Marchmont and would have been prepared to stick things out for twenty years if necessary. One February night Miss Marchmont confides to her the story of her (Miss Marchmont's) lost love. She concludes by telling Lucy that even if we do not understand God we must accept what he does. She resolves to try to make Lucy happy, but she dies before she can do so.

Commentary

This brief chapter is an important one in the structure of the novel. Firstly, Lucy glosses over her life 'at home' but uses an extended sea/tempest metaphor to cover the period: structurally this links with the end of the novel and M.Paul's fate. Lucy appears to have had what would today be called a nervous breakdown. Soon we are to find that this excessive morbidity is a state which occurs later in her life at particular periods. But the Miss Marchmont episode is also a particular plot and structural pointer, for, like her, Lucy is to experience the poignancy of a lost love – or at the very least the fixed obsession that her love is lost. Lucy gives one the impression of being initially sorry for herself, but the concealment of exactly what happened to her in the eight years is undoubtedly an attempt to quicken the narrative pace. The author, like her character, is being selective. Before Miss Marchmont's story there is the 'voice' of the weather – the elements always speak to Lucy (as indeed they did to Charlotte Brontë) and contribute to her moods. Here it is the symbol of great disturbance – it disturbs the past of Miss Marchmont and Lucy's present, and when it dies down Miss Marchmont tells of the great disturbance of her past. What she says has a profound effect upon Lucy and in fact contributes to the crises of her life – for Miss Marchmont puts Frank before God, and Lucy is reduced much later to seeking advice and solace from Père Silas. The duplication of that situation is here in miniature with Miss Marchmont asking Lucy to be her 'chaplain'. The economy of the chapter produces a telling effect on the reader, for Lucy is now again flung on her own resources.

a bark slumbering through halcyon weather . . . the ship was lost, the crew perished The whole of this passage should be studied in some detail. It symbolizes Lucy's struggle with life over a period of time, and the sustained metaphor becomes a fact at the end of the novel with the death – or supposed death – of M.Paul.

I still felt life at life's sources This is another key to Lucy's character. Her outward appearance – which is a 'wan spectacle' – is as nothing compared with her emotional life. This is to become more apparent as her story unfolds.

long mental canker i.e. sustained depression or suffering.

a voice near Miss Marchmont's house This is supernatural and symbolic – just as Jane hears Rochester's 'voice' in *Jane Eyre*, so the voice of the elements here signals the coming disturbance of death and a changed life (for Lucy). It must be added that Lucy often hears voices, generally from within herself.

the legend of the Banshee Scottish/Irish legend that the sound of a wailing spirit beneath the windows heralds a death in the house.

Be my chaplain and tell me The appeal to Lucy anticipates Lucy's appeal in its turn to Père Silas.

Chapter 5
Turning a New Leaf

Lucy, now twenty-three years old, is paid off for her services to Miss Marchmont. By chance she seizes upon the idea of going abroad to make a living. Lucy is very depressed when she arrives in London but succeeds in finding a room which is 'in the shadow of St Paul's' (page 107).

Commentary

Once more the narrative is hurried on, with considering what might-have-been (Miss Marchmont, had she lived, would have provided for Lucy) an important element in Lucy's position and her decision. Chance here is replaced by chance later, for had she not overheard the housekeeper Mrs Barrett and Mrs Leigh talking about Englishwomen in foreign families, Lucy might never have gone abroad. She tells of her journey to London, looking back as an old woman on the past. The atmosphere in London, her bewilderment, her fight to hold on to her common-sense (personified as usual) make the experience immediate, harrowing, lonely. Always Lucy has a keen social awareness, so that she is conscious of the hotel servants and their assessment of her. Lucy suffers – the seven unanswered questions convey her desolation at the thought of what she has done and the lack of certainty of what she must do. But she is tough, determined, brave; she has recourse to prayer, realizes where she is, and takes unvoiced consolation from it.

Still all inward darkness, I left her about twilight One of Charlotte's most distinctive stylistic effects is her ability to produce the tellingly economic contrast, as here.

'Leave this wilderness' This is an inner voice, and Lucy is much given to inward debate.

a Babylon London is often compared to Babylon. The general association is of course with wickedness.

a doubtful state between patronage and politeness Again note the
finely ironic balance of the phrase.

Chapter 6
London

The first part of this chapter reflects the narrator's expressive
delight in the spirit of London. She makes friends with the
waiter, and then goes out into the city and the west end, express-
ing her own preference for the city by which she is 'deeply
excited' (page 109). She gets information about ships which are
to sail for the continent, and she sets off bravely for the wharf on
a dark night. She gets to the ship, 'THE VIVID', and realizes that
she has been cheated yet again, this time by the waterman who
has taken her out to it. The stewardess on the boat is loud and
talkes all night, and the next day Lucy gives an account of the
passengers coming on board. She meets a young English girl
who is sophisticated beyond her years and who reveals a lot
about herself and her school in Belgium. Her name is Ginevra
Fanshawe, and the school she attends is in Villette, the capital of
Labassecour. Ginevra rather looks down on Lucy when she finds
that Lucy has to earn her living. Lucy describes the voyage and
her dream of Europe. Lucy lodges at an inn on arrival at a
sea-port town.

Commentary

The morning produces a complete change of mood in Lucy.
London excites her, and she responds to its challenges by
exploring it. Even the waiter appears to her transformed, and
Lucy discovers that 'Elation and pleasure were in my heart'
(page 109). She reveals that she has an infinite capacity for
experience. In this new state of mind she is intent on accepting
the greater challenge of going abroad, since she has nothing to
tie her to England. We admire her courage and independence in
setting off on this course, and the sense of her own limitations
when she is cheated.

Lucy is a keen observer of people, and on board ship she
observes the stewardess and forms her own conclusions (which
she has to adjust in the light of the woman's later kindness).
Always her imagination works overtime, and she has feelings of

insecurity and uncertainty which she has to fight. The snobbery with regard to the Watsons is noted and, when she meets and listens to Ginevra, we are aware that she is keen-sighted in her appraisal and sees to the heart of the girl's flippancy. Ginevra herself is blatantly egoistic, snobbish too, but is put down in her sea-sickness by the firmness of Lucy. It is this firmness which is to enable Lucy first to survive and then control the girls in Madame Beck's school later. Ginevra's revelations about herself and the school show that she too has her sensitivities. Lucy's dream is further evidence of her imaginative capacity, but she herself destroys it in the interests of what she knows is realism. Yet she expresses regret that her journey is over when they reach port – it has cushioned her for a while from this reality – and the kindness of the stewardess rather surprises her. We have to observe that Lucy is not always right. The chapter ends with Lucy exhausted and depressed at the thought of what may happen – she trembles from apprehension, her sensitive nature once more exposed to the toughness of life.

shook its always-fettering wings half loose A fine natural image to reflect Lucy's change of mood and a new sense of confidence.

Jonah's gourd The plant by which he was shaded (Jonah 4:5–7). It was destroyed the next day.

the eating rust of obscurity A telling metaphor – it underlines Lucy's character and determination, for she is choosing to reject this.

Boue-Marine French port, probably fictitious.

savoir-faire i.e. capacity to do the right thing.

Styx ... Charon ... Land of Shades In Greek legend Charon was the boatman who took the souls of the dead across the river Styx to Hades.

quakerism i.e. the costume is grey-coloured, as worn by Quakers.

jeunes Young.

inconvenant Out of place, not suitable.

blasée i.e. so used to something that you take it for granted.

steerage passengers Those who could only afford the cheapest fare.

"Schönes Mädchen" Beautiful girl.

Labassecour Belgium (literally, farmyard).

mâitresses ... professeurs ... élèves ... au diable Teachers ... professors ... pupils ... to the devil.

'As poor as Job' See the Book of Job 1:6–21.

an officer on half-pay i.e. retired.

Heureusement je sais ... Happily I know how to make the best of things.

Stone walls do not a prison make ... A quotation from 'To Althea from Prison' by Richard Lovelace (1618–58).

Day-dreams are delusions of the demon Again we note Lucy's sudden change of mood, here occasioned by the physical symptom of sea-sickness.

Chapter 7
Villette

Lucy takes stock of her surroundings and ponders whether or not to go to Villette. She is urged to seek out Madame Beck by Ginevra Fanshawe, and sets out for the city in depressing weather and through a depressing countryside. Arriving at a bureau, Lucy finds that she has lost her trunk and asks an Englishman whose voice she has heard to help her locate it. It has been left behind at Boue-Marine, but will be sent on later. She still has some money, and the kindly stranger directs her to an inn. She is accosted on the way by two men, but leaves them behind and comes suddenly upon Madame Beck's establishment. She asks to see Madame Beck, is questioned by one of the latter's staff, and finally studied by M.Paul. He counsels his employer to engage her, and this is done.

Commentary

Lucy surveying the people at the inn displays her usual social sensitivity, feeling that because of her non-status people are looking down on her. Once more she acts on whim, prodded into action by Ginevra Fanshawe's words. The journey is vividly described, and although Lucy says that she enjoys it, the language is redolent of apprehension and fear: the canals are 'like half-torpid green snakes' and she speaks of her anxiety as 'like a tiger crouched in a jungle' (page 122). The loss of the trunk is dramatic, the encounter with the stranger almost romantic: what is superbly conveyed is Lucy's near panic at the loss of her trunk and the gratitude she displays. She also shows courage in pressing on, and such is the nature of the narrative that we fear for her when the men speak insolently to her. Coincidence is stretched in two incidents: firstly her rescue earlier by the unknown Dr John (Graham Bretton); and here by her finding Madame Beck's school instead of the inn. The chapter is written at emotional peak from Lucy's point of view: she goes from crisis to crisis through experience. Already we get hints of Madame

Beck's character in the uncompromising check-ups she carries out on Lucy. We also see too the eccentricity and unpredictable quirkiness of M.Paul in this initial meeting.

marmots Rodents of the squirrel family, here applied to the girls in the school.
Diligence Coach, horse-driven passenger vehicle.
Chaussée Roadway.
'Qu'est ce que vous faîtes donc? . . .' 'What are you doing there? That trunk belongs to me.'
'Pensionnat de Demoiselles' Young Ladies Boarding-School.
shod with the shoes of silence Note how the alliteration superbly conveys the surreptitious secrecy which is to characterize Madame Beck's actions in the future.
maîtresse Mistress, teacher.
Labassecourienne A Belgian.
Albion The ancient poetical name for Britain.
'Il n'y a que les Anglaises . . .' Only Englishwomen would try this kind of thing – how brave those women are.'
'Voilà pour la prière du soir!' 'That (the bell which has just rung) is for evening prayers.'
physiognomy . . . countenance In the nineteenth century much store was placed on appearance and, for example, phrenology, as a way of interpreting character.
'Et qu'en dites vous?' . . . 'Mais – bien des choses,' 'And what do you say about it? . . . Well . . . quite a lot.'
'eh bien! ma cousine, ce sera . . .' 'Well, my cousin, it will always be a good deed.'

Chapter 8
Madame Beck

Lucy has some supper, and is visited again by Madame Beck and shown where she is to sleep. She wakes in the middle of the night to find Madame Beck studying her and examining her things. She removes Lucy's keys and goes away to take wax impressions of them. The next day Madame dismisses Mrs Sweeny, whom Lucy is to replace. The description of Madame Beck shows the imposing nature of her character. There follows an account of the school itself. Madame's system of 'surveillance' and 'espionage' is spelled out, but Lucy pays tribute to her remarkable nature. The garden is also described. Madame Beck senses that Lucy is a natural teacher, and when the opportunity arises places her in front of a class, virtually forcing her into the situation.

Lucy enters on the experience with trepidation but commands discipline by making an example of a pupil.

Commentary

The chapter is dominated by the woman who provides its title. A spy who finds out everything about her staff, she rules through that knowledge and is unruffled in the execution of her office, as she shows in the dismissal of Mrs Sweeny. There is something ominous about this exercise of power, and the night atmosphere is particularly Gothic. But one has to admit that she is strong, well-organised, religious according to her fashion, responsible towards the pupils and appreciates honesty in others. She is of course a hypocrite, and after all her spying Lucy is able to take her own view of her religion (Madame Beck's) and objects to it and its rituals in no uncertain terms. She observes that 'interest was the master-key of madame's nature' (page 136) the perfect image to describe her practice, since she unlocks the secrets of all others either herself or through her spies. Lucy, observing too that a school is too small an area for such a woman, employs considerable irony at her expense. Moreover, Madame Beck is apparently incapable of being moved emotionally. She is too an opportunist, as she demonstrates when she quickly recognizes Lucy's talent for teaching. Lucy herself says that she (Lucy) exists through 'the life of thought, and that of reality' (page 140). When she urges Lucy to take on the class she shows some psychological penetration too – for her exercise of power virtually provokes Lucy into trying to exercise her own. The schoolroom atmosphere is finely conveyed, as is Lucy's courage, which she has to fight to maintain. Her tearing of the exercise plus the incident with Dolores mentioned above show her spirit, and the chapter ends on an ironic note. Lucy has been successful, but Madame Beck has been listening and looking through the peep-hole just to see exactly what happens. In this way the narrative tension is maintained.

sabots Wooden-soled shoes worn by peasants.
face of stone Effective image to express Madame Beck's lack of humanity.
Anglicé or Hibernice i.e. rendered into English.
'chambre d'enfants' Pupils' bedroom.
the head and front of her offending An echo of *Othello* Act I scene 3 –

'true I have married her. The very head and front of my offending/
Hath this extent, no more.

Aurora The goddess of dawn in Roman mythology.

femme de chambre Chambermaid.

Minos The legendary King of Crete who commanded the sacrifice of
young men and women to the minotaur.

Ignacia The female equivalent of Ignatius, and therefore recalling the
Jesuit Ignatius Loyola. This is part of Lucy's anti-Catholic tone.

'souliers de silence' Silent shoes.

alpha and omega Beginning and end.

'Pour les pauvres' For the poor.

Gethsemane . . . death on Calvary For the first see Mark 14:32–42.
The second is of course the crucifixion.

berceau Bower.

jours de sortie i.e. days when outings were undertaken.

gaufres Waffles.

seen through the enchantment of distance An echo of Thomas
Campbell's ''Tis distance lends enchantment to the view.'

Mrs Barbauld's Anna Laetitia Barbauld (1743–1824), writer of prose
for children and also studies of literature.

the hornbook Leaf of paper with alphabet inscribed upon it. It is
mounted on a wooden frame and protected by a thin layer or plate of
horn.

tell it not in Gath See II Samuel 1:20 'don't let your enemies know.'

'Dîtes donc . . . vous sentez vous . . . Tell me . . . do you really feel too
weak (to undertake this)?

'En avant' Forward.

Ce sont les Labassecouriennes . . .' 'These are the Labassecouriennes,
brusque, open, direct and not a little rebellious.'

'C'est vrai' It's quite true.

bonne d'enfants Nursemaid.

ayant l'air de rien Having the appearance of being about to do
something.

Ça ira That will do.

Chapter 9
Isidore

There is a further description of the school and of its mixed
population. The propensity of the Labassecouriennes for lying
is stressed, and Lucy stresses too the difficulties facing her as a
teacher. She gets on well, but soon realizes that as a Protestant
teacher in a Catholic school she is being spied on and reported
on. Ginevra Fanshawe now returns into her life, confiding to her
the fact that she has a suitor whom she christens 'Isidore'. She is

invited out by her wealthy friend Mrs Cholmondeley, and shows off before Lucy. Ginevra also reveals that the jewellery she is wearing has been given to her as a present. The person who gave it to her was 'Isidore', who thinks her perfect. She of course has other male friends, and Lucy reprimands her for 'deceiving' Isidore. Ginevra tells Lucy that she much prefers her other lover, 'Le Colonel Alfred de Hamal.' (page 156).

Commentary

Lucy's own appraisal of her pupils is incisively expressed, her opinion being that often the commoner is better bred than the aristocrat. She records her own struggles, but her will-power causes her to triumph over the pupils she terms 'mutineers' (page 146). She treats them with what we should call a psychological soundness by a considered application to their characters; the uncertainty of her position is however obvious when, after achieving popularity, she is spied upon and even condoled with for being a Protestant. Ginevra Fanshawe's superficialities are further investigated and exposed, but we do get the impression that Lucy envies her prettiness. Consequently her accounts of Ginevra are conditioned by a prejudice and also, despite herself, by a wish to know more about the mysterious 'Isidore'. Lucy has a degree of Puritanism in her make-up which causes her to consider the present of the jewels with distaste. Ginevra is vain and silly, but even when she is talking her nonsense in French we see why 'Isidore' is fascinated by her. Lucy, however, always has sufficient character to recognize her arrogance, and she can be firm with her too.

'J'ai menti plusieurs fois' 'I have lied many times.'
Imprimis In the first place.
'Dieu que c'est difficile! . . .' 'God knows this is difficult! I want no
   more to do with it. It wearies me.'
she who ran might read An echo of 'he that runs may read' by the
   eighteenth century poet William Cowper (1731–1800).
'Parceque, quand vous serez morte . . .' 'Because, when you are dead
   you will burn in the fires of Hell.'
'Croyez-vous?' 'Do you believe that?'
'Certainement que j'y crois . . .' 'Assuredly I believe it; all the world
   knows it; and moreover the priest has told me this.'
'Pour assurer votre salut là-haut . . .' 'To make sure of your salvation
   above, they would be wise to burn you down here.'

'**Comme cela . . . Ça suffit**' 'So, so . . . that's good enough.'

'**a ce qu'on dit**' 'As they say'.

beau, mais plutôt bel homme . . .' Handsome, but rather a fine man than an attractive one.

ceinture beau celeste A sky-blue sash.

Diogenes The Greek philosopher (c.400–325 BC), a cynic who practised austerity in Athens.

'**On est là pour**' 'Someone is here to see . . .'

'**Ecoutez, chère grogneuse**' 'Listen dear grumbler.'

blanc-bec Greenhorn, unsophisticated and inexperienced person.

'**Mais pas du tout! . . . Je suis sa reine . . .**' 'Not at all! . . . I am his queen, but he is not my king.'

'**Les penseurs, les hommes profonds et passionés . . .**' The thinkers, the deep and impassioned men, are not to my taste . . . I go for the handsome fops and the attractive scoundrels. Long live joys and pleasures. Down with noble passions and strict virtues!

'**J'aime mon beau colonel**' 'I love my handsome colonel.'

'**Je n'aimerai jamais son rival . . .**' 'I will never love his rival. Me, I will never be the wife of a bourgeois.'

Chapter 10
Dr John

The distant behaviour of Madame Beck to her own children is described, for although she is concerned for them, she never shows them any affection. The younger daughter Fifine has an accident one day, and instead of the regular Dr Pillule, a young doctor comes to see her. Lucy describes him and observes that he speaks English very well. She also reveals that this is the man who had helped her recover her missing trunk. Thereafter he often comes to visit the child and then her elder sister, who is not really ill, and Madame Beck seems to be intent on cultivating his acquaintance more intimately. Lucy herself studies him intently, and this draws forth a comment from him.

Commentary

The coldness of Madame Beck's nature is indicated in her attitude to her children, but this also partakes of a particular blindness with regard to faults. The actions of Désirée reflect the lack of maternal affection given to her (and also perhaps the lack of a father, as he is dead). Madame Beck's deviousness in dealing with this child is of a piece with her other hypocrisies. The accident to Fifine provides drama, with Dr John evincing a very good bedside manner and sympathetic approach to his young patient. There is an interesting interaction between Madame Beck and Dr John, her flattery of him and her reception of him being, in anyone of less imposing character, what we would call flirtation. His attitude to her seems to be one of ironic amusement, as if he deliberately goes along with what she is doing but knows, certainly in the case of Désirée's fake illness and Madame's silent connivance here, what is the truth of the matter. He decides, as Lucy puts it, 'to play his part in the farce' (page 162). At the same time we note that Dr John is able to preserve his independence and is in no way guilty of currying favour. Although Lucy identifies him as the stranger at the bureau, we sense that there is an even more positive identification nagging at the back of her mind. This arouses expectation in the reader. Typically, Lucy, questioned directly by Dr John, does not answer, and the chapter ends on a note of mystery.

'leur avenir' i.e. what they would become.
'Prends garde, mon enfant!' 'Take care, my child!'
'Quelle peste que cette Désirée! ...' 'What a pest is that Désirée! What a trial that child is!'
beaufet Sideboard.
salle à manger Dining room.
'Désirée a besoin ...' 'Désirée needs to have a particular watch kept on her.'
'Cet enfant a un os cassé' 'This child has a broken bone.'
'et qu'on aille tout ...' 'and someone go and look for a cab immediately.'
eau sucrée Water sweetened with sugar.
gourmande Someone who loves eating.
'Ça vaudra mieux' 'That will do better' (in reference to the steadiness of Madame Beck's hand).
'Merci madame: très bien ... Voilà un sang-froid ...' 'Thank you Madame: very good — very good indeed ... That was a very appropriate coolness, and worth a thousand expressions of misguided sensibility.'
Dutch-made women i.e. stolid and heavily built.
empressement Readiness.
which Nebuchadnezzar the king had set up See Daniel 3:1–7.
the force of surprise, and also of conviction Lucy's suspicions prove to be well-founded, though it takes time for confirmation.

Chapter 11
The Portresse's Cabinet

With the youngest of Madame Beck's children ill, Dr John's visits
to the pensionnat are encouraged. Madame allows him to treat
some of the girls, and silences gossip and parental objections
firmly and tactfully. She herself takes great trouble over her
appearance when she receives him. He handles the situation with
some humour and discretion. On one occasion he comes to visit
the child Georgette. Lucy standing by a door hears 'a giddy treble
laugh' (page 168) and afterwards sees a somewhat disconcerted
Dr John leave the room. She concludes that he has been dismissed
by the French servant Rosine Matou. When Madame Beck
appears she comments on Dr John's health, as if he has been
overworking. Lucy observes that this may be because he has been
upset by something. When he leaves Madame is morose and
discovers that she has one white hair. Lucy meanwhile ponders on
the attractions of the grisette Rosine and finds time to commend
Madame on her ability, after this passing lapse, to behave well.

Commentary

There is an interesting narrative and almost humorous tension in
this chapter. Madame Beck shows her inclination towards Dr
John but does not pass the bounds of discretion, and her handling
of the parents and her capacity to be in control of the situation all
the time reflects her genuine strength. We always get the feeling
that she will not expose herself to damaging criticism, and we also
sense that while she herself is drawn to Dr John she will not let the
situation get out of hand. There is no way that her power will be
reduced. Lucy's suspicions point to the fact that Dr John is trying
to have an affair with Rosine, but the idea of this is sufficiently
vague to make us feel that Lucy is mistaken. Again there is a kind
of ironic humour in the discomfort of Dr John, an indication of
his inclination which is to be explained later as the plot unfolds, or
at least this aspect of it. Lucy has a commendable honesty though,
and despite the fact that she does not like Madame Beck she
acknowledges her strength of character in putting her feelings
down. Her appraisal of Rosine, on the other hand, smacks of
snobbery and sexual jealousy.

Bonne-Maman Grandma

little Jesuit though she might be Lucy is determinedly and provocatively anti-Catholic, and capable of putting it in extremes, as here.

'brava!' i.e. bravo.

'rondeur et franchise de bonne femme' 'Bluntness and freedom of the good wife.'

'ce cher jeune homme! . . .' 'this dear young man! The best creature in all the world!'

voilà tout! That's all!

philoprogenitiveness i.e. of loving their children.

deshabille i.e. untidiness of dress.

brodequins laced boots

'fraîchë brisë and 'Venisë.' 'fresh breeze . . . Venice.'

grisette French working girl (originally, dressed in grey).

trop bonne Very good.

an Apollyon The fearful monster who fights Christian in John Bunyan's *The Pilgrim's Progress* (1678).

Chapter 12
The Casket

This opens with a description of the garden behind the house and also gives an account of the legend of the black and white nun. Lucy herself seeks solitude in this garden, and often walks there in the evenings. The Catholic household are at prayer on one such evening when Lucy walks in the forbidden alley attracted by its loneliness and seeks out the hidden seat which she has cleaned for herself. Lucy contemplates the moon, and thinks back to her childhood, recalling how accidents of weather and atmosphere always disturbed her. She stresses here her longings and the need to be given direction, but on this particular night she is filled 'with a mood of hope' (page 176). Lucy hears a sound and discovers a box, opens it and reads a love-letter, in which she is referred to disparagingly. The only clue to the identity of the writer is his reference to the grey dress. Meanwhile Rosine comes into the garden, and then Dr John comes, obviously searching for the casket (box) which Lucy holds in her hands. Dr John asks Lucy not to betray 'her'. Lucy agrees to remain silent about the affair if Dr John can assure her that none of the girls is involved. Before he can answer they see Madame Beck coming. Dr John disappears before she has seen him (supposedly), but Lucy, pondering later, believes that Madame Beck knows exactly what went on in the garden that night.

Commentary

An important chapter which prepares us for the mysterious happenings with regard to the 'nun', and it is also an index to Lucy's character – she is sensitive, moody, somewhat mystical, very much a prey to atmosphere, as she admits. The need for loneliness is also typical of her character, and her need to establish herself in solitary and contemplative state is pre-eminent. We note too her feeling of being an outsider – in terms of race, religion and temperament – from those with whom she works. The atmosphere of the garden and particularly of the alley, is finely and sympathetically conveyed. In a sense, Lucy using the alley is a mark of her independence. Her thinking back to her childhood is pathos, her reaction to the storm earlier a note of her mystical and vital nature. There is established a Gothic atmosphere, but the arrival of the casket, though it contributes to this, also has a melodramatic and mysterious effect, almost as if the author is here superimposing melodrama on realism – the realism of Lucy's character and consciousness. We note too the fact that Lucy herself has never been singled out for Dr John's smiles, so that there is an irony in her being singled out here as having some power over him. The letter itself is almost a parody of a love-letter in its excesses, though it is effective in prolonging the mystery. The narrative verve is maintained. Lucy does feel some compassion for Dr John (she obviously feels some interest in him too), but the dominating and ominous presence of Madame Beck, who is aware of the true situation, maintains the tension and the mystery. We do not know who the letter was written to!

A vague tale went of a black and white nun An important reference in terms of Lucy's later experiences, and also a contributory factor in setting the Gothic atmosphere of some of the scenes in the novel.
Methuselah See Genesis 5:27. This records that he lived for 969 years.
salut Greeting.
l'allée défendue The forbidden alley.
cuisinière Kitchen-maid.
'comme elle est propre . . .' 'Lucy? Do you really love this place, miss?'
'C'est juste . . . bonté' 'That's right . . . goodness.'
catalepsy The state where the motions of the body are suspended, and the person appears to be in a trance.
Jael to Sisera Judges 4:1–24. Sisera, a commander, had oppressed the Israelites but, being overcome and fleeing, he took shelter with Jael,

wife of Heber, who killed him by driving a tent-peg into his skull.

Heber See previous note.

Pour la robe grise For the grey dress.

billet-doux Love letter.

une véritable bégueule Britannique . . . Truly a British prude from what you say, something of a monster, sharp and rough like a corporal of the grenadiers, and as cross-grained as a nun. (Note particularly the last comparison, which is part of the structure, a kind of running sub-text to the mysterious part of the plot).

Peri Fairy, beautiful being.

la robe grise . . . The grey dress, the straw hat.

'Quel conte! . . .' 'What a tale . . . there wasn't anybody there.'

la brise du soir The evening breeze.

'Quel belle nuit! . . .' 'What a beautiful night . . . how pleasant it is, how fresh the air is.'

'Bon soir, ma bonne amie . . .' 'Good night, my good friend, sleep well.'

Chapter 13
A Sneeze Out of Season

The next morning Lucy goes into the alley to cover up the traces of the previous night's activities. There follows her account of the period of religious study for her pupils in the evenings, and how she finds these evenings so intolerable that she feels she must escape from the building. Lucy goes up to the dormitory and sees Madame Beck sorting through the contents of her (Lucy's) work-box; she decides not to confront Madame because she wants to avoid a scene, and in any case does not wish to lose her employment. Lucy feels that she is confirmed in her suspicions that Madame saw Dr John in the garden. Next day she is calm again, and ponders the reason for Dr John being in the garden. Lucy also feels that Madame suspects that there is something between herself and the doctor. Later she hears Rosine discussing the affair of the garden with Dr John. She sees the latter give Rosine a coin, and, while the doctor is with his young patient, Lucy also sees another billet flutter down from one of the windows into the garden. Dr John orders Lucy to go and pick it up, and when she brings it to him he destroys it. Lucy learns from him that it has been dropped by someone who is writing to one of the girls – and obviously, from what he says, Dr John feels strongly for the girl. Lucy offers him her help to watch over the girl, but just as Dr John is about to tell her who it is they are interrupted by the click of Madame Beck's door followed by a sneeze. She has obviously been eavesdropping on their conversation.

Commentary

The evening study and Lucy's oppression again mark her anti-Catholic stance, an attitude which takes on the form of fanatical objection. She had to use much restraint in order to avoid denouncing the 'lecture pieuse' (page 185), and also to avoid a confrontation with Madame as she searches her belongings. In fact the emphasis in this chapter is on Madame's ability to make sure she finds out what is going on, though the give-away sneeze has a humorous quality for the reader. There is something in Lucy which makes her rather admire the superb organization of Madame's duplicity, and she is able to laugh at the suspicions which link her romantically in Madame's mind with Dr John. But that laughter gives way to a conflict of emotions which, though they are not defined by Lucy, indicate her own feelings for Dr John. Typically, her resilience leads her to a balanced view the next day. Madame's going out – only to return and spy – is further evidence of her suspicions of Lucy. Much of the chapter depends on the half-truths as learned from eavesdropping, and there is a sympathetic exchange between Dr John and Lucy in which she sublimates her own love for him by agreeing to help him. The edge of mystery remains, the sneeze a comic climax which frustrates revelation.

'Etude du soir' Evening study.
'la lecture pieuse' Religious talk.
Intellect . . . Reason . . . Common Sense Note how the heavy personifications convey the weight of Lucy's bias against Catholicism.
gasconading Boastful.
Conrad and Elizabeth of Hungary Conrad was the severe spiritual guide of Elizabeth of Hungary (1207–31), who was the saint celebrated for her charities to the poor.
Mause Headrigg . . . Sergeant Bothwell Two of the characters in Sir Walter Scott's historical novel, *Old Mortality* (1816).
'lits d'ange' Beds of angels.
'unhasting yet unresting' The words are associated with the German philosopher and poet, Johann Wolfgang von Goethe (1749–1832).
it was the rock struck, and Meribah's waters . . . See Exodus 17: 6–7. Moses struck the rock and the water gushed out. He named the place Massah and Meribah.

'Cette enfant a toujours . . .' 'That child always has a touch of fever . . . Has Dr John seen her lately? Am I right in thinking that he hasn't?'
pour faire quelques courses en fiacre i.e. to do some shopping.
Light-heart the Beggar From the tenth satire of Juvenal, Dryden's translation.
chapeau vert tendre Delicate green hat.
malgré maman and médecin In spite of your mother and the doctor.
'Le marmot n'a rien . . .' 'There's nothing the matter with the brat, is there? Not much . . . well then.'
a coup de vent i.e. as quick as the wind.
'Mais enfin' But anyway.
'Ah ça! . . . pour vos frais' 'Ah, well, there is nothing at the back of it – no mystery, no love affair, for example?'
   'No more than you can see in my hand.'
   'What a pity – and I was just beginning to get ideas about that.'
   'Truly, you have got something for your pains.'
'moue' Pout.
a pie A magpie.
duenna Chaperon.
this pearl of great price See *Othello* Act 5 Scene 2:
   Like the base Indian, threw a pearl away
   Richer than all his tribe.
enrhumée . . . i.e. she had a cold.

Chapter 14
The Fête

This long chapter is broken up into a number of sequences. Firstly, Lucy describes three of the teachers, and then the preparations for the event. M.Paul makes his appearance as the producer of the play, while Lucy comments on his behaviour. Suddenly she is approached by him (and persuaded) to take a part in the 'vaudeville' on the special day. Lucy shows her obstinacy, for although she is given a man's part, she refuses to wear masculine clothes on stage thus causing chaos and disagreement. As a result she falls out with Mademoiselle de St Pierre. During the performance she watches her fellow actors – particularly Ginevra Fanshawe – and, in the audience, Dr John. Despite herself, Lucy enjoys her own acting, and afterwards M.Paul is kind to her. At the ball which follows Lucy has a long conversation with Ginevra, who tells her that both her (Ginevra's) suitors are there. Lucy picks out the dandified de Hamal and then realizes, because of his solicitousness, that Dr John is Isidore. Lucy soon gives Ginevra her opinion of both men. Later

Lucy meets Dr John, who asks her to watch over Ginevra for
him. They discuss de Hamal. It is obvious that Dr John is blind
to Ginevra's true nature.

Commentary

Early in the chapter we are given an insight into Madame's
ability to sum up character in her appraisal of the Parisienne,
while Lucy too demonstrates the quality of her own knowledge
of character. There is more anti-Catholic rhetoric from Lucy
('Lucifer just offers the same terms' – page 196). Note the irony
with which Madame's presentation is described. M.Paul tends to
dominate the proceedings in this chapter, at least until the final
sequence between Lucy and Dr John. M.Paul is vividly and
individualistically described. There is some fine description of
the preparations for the day, while the atmosphere of excite-
ment has its comic elements, seen in the girls and teachers going
down to breakfast 'in dressing-gowns and curlpapers' (page
199). Lucy's own transformation at the hands of the hairdresser
occasions her some amazement. Lucy herself mocks the
elaboration of the preparations, while her own sensitivity is seen
in her adopting a 'gown of shadow' (page 200). Madame shows
what we suspect is her hypocrisy by commending Lucy. The
latter typically seeks some refuge in reading, while M.Paul's
power, presence and individual magnetism disturb her as she
studies and dreams. It is a significant moment, for his strength
of personality compels Lucy to listen. In reaction to Lucy's
reading he shows his fiery, critical and perfectionist nature. He
also shows his individual approach to improving Lucy's delivery
by confining her to the attic. There is even something of sadistic
pleasure in his leaving her so long, but Lucy's courage is not in
question. There is method in M.Paul's extremism – he gets the
best out of Lucy and gives her increased confidence. When he
offers her his hand it is symbolic of their later coming together.
It is M.Paul who introduces her to the rest and, when he sees
that she is obstinate and sensitive, helps her to get through the
ordeal. The actual performance does not dull Lucy's observation, particularly with regard to Ginevra. For us – and Lucy –
the revelation is her ability to act, but this is put down by her own
puritanical tendencies, seen in her deliberate renunciation of
such delights. She gives them up for ever – 'the lock of a

resolution which neither Time nor Temptation has since picked.' (page 211). In like mood she also refuses to dance at all, even with M.Paul, who has obviously greatly impressed her. The strictness of the ballroom surveillance is virtually shared between M.Paul and Madame Beck in their different severities. Madame Beck even threatens some of the attendant young men with the ghostly nun. Once more she displays her psychological power by getting the parents on her side, strengthening her own position with them by her unswerving authority. Moody, vain, spoiled – all this is reflected in the behaviour of Ginevra. She patronizes Lucy but cannot do without her support, though Lucy's criticism does her no harm. Ginevra is an unashamed snob. We share Lucy's contempt for the diminutive de Hamal, who is a deliberate physical contrast with Dr John. Ginevra enjoys teasing them, playing them off against each other. Lucy's own unconscious feelings for Dr John are shown in the berating she gives 'the mannikin' (page 218) to Ginevra's face. So impassioned is she that she keeps a fast hold on Ginevra. Lucy's exchanges with Dr John show how besotted that man is with Ginevra. They also show that Lucy's own feelings for him make her restrained, compassionate and considerate in her dealings with him. She even, perhaps misguidedly, gives him some hope.

'Je sais bien qu'elle . . .' 'I know only too well that she has no principles and probably no morals . . . her conduct in class is inevitably proper and even conveys a certain dignity: that is all that is needed. Neither the pupils nor the parents expect more; nor, therefore, do I.'

Lucifer Satan.

'All this power will I give thee . . .' Luke 4:6–7. The temptation of Christ after the forty days in the wilderness.

'grand berceau' Large bower.

'Vite!' Quick.

'Eh bien! Deux ou trois . . .' 'Very good. Two or three silver spoons and forks.'

'Ecoutez!' 'Listen!'

'Vous n'êtes donc que des poupées? . . .' 'You are merely dolls, then? Have you no passions? Don't you feel anything? Your flesh is snow, your blood is made of ice. Me, I want everything to be all right, so that it has life and spirit.'

'avec délices' With delight.

coiffeur Hairdresser.

bénitier One who blesses.

tailleuse Seamstress.

'si triste . . .' 'So sombre – so lacking in display.'

kept me in countenance Observed me.

'convenablement' ... Properly, discreetly, with propriety and decency.

'des femmes mûres ...' 'Mature women ... as for that St Pierre, she has the appearance of an old coquette pretending to be an inexperienced girl.

'C'est cela!' ... 'That's it. I know her: it is the Englishwoman. It doesn't matter. As she is English, and therefore completely narrow-minded, she will do what I require, or I will know why.'

moyens Means.

minauderies Simperings.

amour-propre Pride.

Dieu sait que je les déteste ... God knows that in the ordinary course of things, I hate them like the plague.

'Vîte à l'ouvrage!' 'Quickly to work!'

'Ça ira!' 'Let us go!'

fat Fop.

apropos Appropriately.

'J'ai tout entendu ... A bas la timidité!' 'I've heard everything. It will do. Repeat it. Again. And no sour expressions. Get rid of your diffidence.'

'Enfin, elle le sait,' 'At least she knows it.'

'J'ai bien faim ..' 'I am very hungry.'
   'What, you're hungry! And what about the meal?'
   'Ah, that's true.'

bonne bouche Literally good mouthful, a treat.

'A la bonne heure' That's right.

Blue-beard The wealthy castle-owner of legend who had killed his previous wives: the last one discovers them, but is rescued by her brothers.

'N'est-ce pas que ...' Isn't it beautiful?

'De l'ordre!' Order!

halte là! Stop there!

petit-maître Little man.

vaudeville de pensionnat School entertainment.

'Courage, mon ami! ... 'Courage, my friend. A little self-possession, a little nerve, Mr Lucy and everything will go well.'

erst Previously (archaic).

'C'est, peutêtre plus beau ...' 'It may perhaps be better than your model ... but it isn't quite right.'

the yearned-for seasoning Note the image, for Lucy often uses connected images. Later she says of Ginevra, 'she tasted a condiment'.

'jeunes gens' Young people.

'belle blonde' ... 'jolie brune' Beautiful blonde ... pretty brunette.

'cette jeune fille magnifique ....' 'That wonderful girl with the jet-black hair.

'Taisez-vous! ... la nonnette du jardin.' 'Shut up. You will not pass me unless it is over my dead body, and you will only dance with the nun in the garden.

like a little Buonaparte . . . i.e. Napoleon Bonaparte, celebrated French general and emperor, finally defeated by the Prussians and the British at Waterloo (1815).

'Sortez, sortez . . .' 'Get out, get out, and as quickly as possible.'

poor outcast Cain See Genesis 4: 11–16.

'The murder is out' 'The secret is revealed.'

'C'est lui-même . . . oh, ciel!' 'That is certainly him . . . O heavens!'

'cela suffit . . .' 'That's enough. I don't want him.'

'Mars . . . Apollo' The first the God of war in Roman mythology, the second the sun-god of Greek and Roman mythology associated with poetry and music.

kennel Gutter.

Chapter 15
The Long Vacation

This opens with an account of the 'cram' for the examination, with M.Paul officiating on the fateful day, taking over everything except English, which he hasn't mastered. Lucy walks in the garden and is joined by M.Paul. After some teasing repartee, he shakes hands with her and the next day he makes her part in the examination easy. Everyone leaves as the holidays begin, and Lucy suffers the extremity of loneliness, her only companion being a cretin. When the latter goes, Lucy tries to imagine what her term-time companions are doing. Eventually she becomes so depressed that she takes to her bed, experiencing a terrible fever and fear. She does not call the doctor but goes one evening to a church, and sees the priest in the confessional, who is moved by her outpouring and tries to convert her to Catholicism. The priest asks her to call on him the next day, but she clearly sees that although he is kind he will try to convert her to his faith. Lucy tries to get back to the pensionnat through a storm, but collapses near a large building.

Commentary

There are more insights into the character of M.Paul (for example his resentment of display in anyone except himself). Lucy is ironic about the preparations of the other teachers, and distances herself from the examination experience as far as she can. But we note that Lucy's relationship with M.Paul is a deepening one, and his mercurial nature is reflected in his shaking hands with Lucy. The latter's loneliness becomes a psychological state and, despite her attempts to be independent, there is little doubt that she is only so in these circumstances by force of will. 'My heart almost died within me' (page 227) reflects the desolation of her mood. Invocation to the reader is followed by prayers as her depression deepens. The walks Lucy takes after the cretin has gone are physically debilitating, and this complements her morbidity. Lucy becomes suicidal, but in her mania (and delirium) envies Ginevra Fanshawe for having inspired a loyal love. She passes through fever into a waking despair about the future. Her visit to the priest is filled with Lucy's own prejudices, and she senses that although he is a good man he is inadequate to deal with her own needs. Charlotte Brontë here shows her psychological penetration however, for it is the comfort of release which Lucy gains. There is something facile in the way the priest translates Lucy's suffering into a divine message, to bring her back to the true church. Lucy's suspicions are heightened. The chapter ends on the high dramatic note of her collapse.

'année scolaire' School year.
like those of a wrathful cat Typical of M.Paul, who often waits to pounce verbally.
'Ainsi . . . ambitieuse!' 'Thus . . . you will be enthroned like a queen – enthroned by my side. Doubtless you are tasting in advance the delights of authority. I believe that I see in you some kind of radiance, you ambitious little creature.'
'une de ses beautés' One of his attractions.
'Que vous etes dûr, monsieur!' 'How unyielding you are, sir!'
'je me tins . . .' 'I took it for a warning.'
'par exemple . . .' 'for example, the son, the moon, the stars – did I say that correctly?'
'Donnez-moi la main,' 'Give me your hand.'
'Pauvrette!' Poor little thing.
'Mon père, je suis protestante.' 'Father, I am Protestant.'
Babylonish furnace i.e. symbolic of Hell and evil.
Fénélon François Fénélon (1651–1715) French religious writer who directed a seminary for female converts to Catholicism, hence Lucy's association here.

Revision questions on Chapters 1–5

1 Write an account of Lucy's life before she goes to Villette.

2 In what ways are Madame Beck and Ginevra Fanshawe dominated by self-interest?

3 What ideas have you formed about Lucy's character? Refer to the text in your answer.

4 What do you consider to be the most dramatic scene in the novel so far and why?

5 Compare and contrast M. Paul and Dr John as they appear in these chapters.

6 With particular reference to three or four incidents, show how Charlotte Brontë manages to convey a convincing atmosphere.

Volume Two
Chapter 16
Auld Lang Syne

When Lucy finally comes round she realizes that she is in a house, to be specific she is in 'a pleasant parlour' (page 238), where she gradually begins to recognize some of the furniture. Lucy feels that she is back amid the scenes of her girlhood, and even temporarily entertains the idea that she is dreaming. She takes a sleeping draught and when she wakes this time believes that she is back in Bretton. Lucy finds her own initials on a pin-cushion, but when she looks outside she does not know where she is. She recognizes a portrait of Graham and remembers lifting Paulina up to see it. Then she finds that Mrs Bretton is at her bedside. With the arrival of Dr John, really Graham Bretton, we learn that Lucy's earlier suspicions are here confirmed, for 'its dawn had penetrated my perceptions long since' (page 247), though she says that she deliberately kept these suspicions to herself. Mrs Bretton realizes that she is Lucy, but Graham is much slower to realize. They bring each other up to date with their news, and Lucy feels that she is among friends.

Commentary

There is some fine atmospheric writing here, though the plot pivot of identity is not convincing. Lucy's excuse for keeping quiet about what she has suspected is only acceptable when we consider the withdrawn nature of her character. The fact that Mrs Bretton has spotted the likeness makes it all the more incredible that Graham Bretton has to be prompted into recognizing Lucy. Nevertheless we realize that Lucy has passed through a crisis and that the practical goodness of the Brettons is much more reassuring and morale-lifting to her than any spiritual sustenance offered by a Catholic priest.

Memory . . . Spirit . . . Substance The personifications emphasize
   Lucy's heightened state, almost of delirium.
Bedridden Hassan . . . gates of Damascus This is a reference to a
   character in *The Arabian Nights* who becomes a pastry-cook in
   Damascus.
Lares Household Gods, valued possessions.
I had preferred to keep the matter to myself And in doing so, thus
   conveniently producing the plot revelation here. But such secrecy is
   typical of Lucy.

Chapter 17
La Terrasse

The chapter opens with a sermon to the reader. Lucy is too weak to get up, so Mrs Bretton comes to sit beside her. Mrs Bretton has been instructed by Graham not to let Lucy overtax herself. Lucy dreams throughout the day and, when Graham comes, he tells her about the 'quiet little chateau' (page 255) where they are. Graham also tells her that he has carried the news to the pensionnat that she is safe. Graham asks Lucy if she is a Catholic, and tells her how he came to find her the previous night through the agency of the old priest. Lucy in return confides her own state of mind to him, and Graham tells her how he and Père Silas cared for her. All the time Lucy is aware of Graham's feelings for Ginevra Fanshawe.

Commentary

Notice the vividness of Lucy's imagination, particularly when she comes round, and her subconscious while she is dreaming.

Vivid sea imagery, symbolic of her restless state, dominates the language she uses. We are aware that her own love for Graham is in abeyance, though she is touched by his having thought of her. The substance of the chapter fills in the detail of the previous night. Graham shows his concern for Lucy by stressing that she should have had a holiday. We notice the delightful understanding between mother and son, though Lucy is so sensitive on Graham's account that she knows his mother would disapprove of Ginevra.

the waiting waters will stir See John 5:2 The pool is Bethesda.
Azrael Angel of death mentioned in the Koran.
cuisinière Kitchen-maid.
Hypochondria Heavily personified to indicate the extent of Lucy's depression.
Titania . . . Bottom The Queen of the fairies and the weaver she temporarily falls in love with in Shakespeare's *A Midsummer Night's Dream*.
Benjamin's portion Joseph gave Benjamin much more than any of his other brothers (Genesis 43:34).

Chapter 18
We Quarrel

As Lucy anticipated, Graham begins to talk of Ginevra, calling her Lucy's friend, and cross-questioning her in order to confirm his own estimation of Ginevra. Fed up with his delusions over Ginevra, Lucy angrily tells him of them. In the evening Lucy finds some difficulty in approaching Graham, though he is kind to her. Eventually, when they are left alone, Lucy apologizes for her impetuous words of that morning. Graham forgives her and their quarrel is over. There is a natural warmth established between them, Lucy having indicated her respect for Graham and he having shown a genuine generosity of response. Lucy has to hear much of Ginevra, and enters so far into Graham's situation as to assert that Ginevra will accept him one day, though she knows in her heart that this is not true. She says that Ginevra will repay his gifts to her, but she senses, when she looks closely at Dr John, that perhaps he does see into Ginevra despite what he says.

Commentary

The chapter reveals the impetuosity of Lucy's nature and her humility and genuine repentance when she realizes how rude she has been to Graham. What is intriguing here is the depth with which Lucy is presented by Charlotte Brontë, for she plays Devil's advocate in the sense of encouraging Graham to believe that he will ultimately succeed with Ginevra. Whether this is because of her own feelings for Dr John, or whether it is that she is trying to draw some response from him, it is difficult to say. There are indications that there is more depth to Dr John, that he has his own doubts, which he is not prepared to utter, about Ginevra. Lucy is a teasing little hypocrite here, and this spirited probing shows how much better in health she is. She was right when she said that she needed companionship.

Chapter 19
The Cleopatra

Lucy stays on at La Terrasse for a fortnight after term begins. Madame comes to visit her, and gushes about the place and about Mrs Bretton, for she is 'quite a living catherine-wheel of compliments, delight, and affability.' (page 270). Every day Lucy spends with the Brettons is happy because of the little arrangements which they make. Lucy gives a dual portrait of Graham Bretton in his public and private life; she also indicates his great, encompassing knowledge of Villette. Lucy dwells on the visits to the picture galleries where one particular picture (called *Cleopatra*) absorbs her attention. While Lucy is studying the picture, M.Paul taps her on the shoulder. He is surprised that she is alone and appalled that she is viewing this picture. Lucy continues viewing more pictures, and then has another conversation with M.Paul. He asks her about the vacation, and spells out what he thinks are the contradictions in her nature. When Lucy asks Dr John about the *Cleopatra* he refuses to 'Compare that mulatto with Ginevra!' (page 282).

Commentary

This superb chapter first focuses on Madame Beck and her facilely gushing behaviour when she visits the Brettons: Lucy sees into Madame Beck's real feelings when she finds her sitting stonily in the carriage. Lucy dwells on the character of Graham Bretton, and his efforts on behalf of the poor particularly excite her sympathy and our interest though, despite what she says, we feel that he may be too good to be true. Graham's private portrait finds Lucy aware, however, of his vanity and his natural wish to receive homage: she also notices his need to repay, hence the daily consideration he shows her in terms of trips into Villette and its art galleries. Lucy in her appraisal of art shows the individual independence we have come to expect from her. She realizes that masterpieces are very rare, and does not hesitate to attack the fat women of Flemish art. There may be a psychological reason for this: Lucy could hardly be described as voluptuous, and it may be that she has a fear of the flesh, of full-blooded sexuality represented in the paintings. Certainly there is an implication here that the pictures are for men. But if there is some jealousy of the Cleopatra, there is certainly much humour too, and plenty of emphasis on the sordid details which give the title its irony. M.Paul, despite his Catholicism, seems to be puritanical about Lucy looking at such a picture, while Lucy's account of the four 'Anges' is another expression not only of her taste in art but of her determined anti-Catholicism. M.Paul himself employs effective irony at Lucy's expense, but he also shows his interest in her and something of his own passionate nature. There is considerable chemistry between them. A series of exclamations express Lucy's opinion of de Hamal, but the sense of running contrasts is maintained when Dr John looks at the Cleopatra. In fact the scene has placed all three men in contradistinction to one another.

'une pièce magnifique . . . tellement dignes, aimables, et
  respectables . . . A magnificent room . . . dignified to a degree,
  pleasant and respectable.
'madame sa mère . . ' Your mother, the dignified mistress of the house.
a living catherine-wheel A superbly imaginitave image.
'Open! Sesame.' Another *Arabian Nights* reference – the password that
  opens everything.
cicerone The guide who shows and explains the antiquities.
chef d'ouevres Masterpieces.
'Que faites vous ici?' . . . 'de l'autre coté.' 'What are you doing here?'
  'Sir, I am amusing myself.'
  'Amusing yourself! And with what, if you please? But first, do me
  the favour of getting up. Take my arm, and let us go to the other side.'
'Singulières femmes . . .' 'How extraordinary Englishwomen are!'

'Taisez-vous . . . là!' 'Shut up and sit down there – there!'

'Mais, mademoiselle . . . quels laids tableaux!' 'But, miss, sit down and don't budge, do you hear, until someone comes to look for you or until I give my permission.'

   'What a sad corner . . . and what ugly pictures!'

'La vie d'une femme' . . . 'Jeune Fille' 'Mariée' 'Jeune Mère' 'Veuve' . . . Anges 'The life of a woman' . . . 'Young Woman' 'Wife . . .' 'Young mother . . . Widow . . . Angels.'

'Vraiment! . . . chose.' 'In truth, you are not worth much.'

'Cela ne vaut rien . . . de sa côté.' 'That matters but little – a superb woman with an imperial and Junoesque figure, but not the kind of person I would want in a wife, nor a daughter, nor a sister. You will not look even once more in that direction.'

Nebuchadnezzar's hottest furnace Daniel 3, where the miraculous deliverance was responsible for converting the Babylonian tyrant to Judaism.

Venus of the Nile i.e. Cleopatra.

acerb i.e. sour looking.

Hesperides The nymphs who were daughters of Hesperus, guardians of the garden where the golden apples grew in the Islands of the Blessed.

tractable Arabian . . . stubborn 'sheltie.' i.e. the finely bred Arabian horse and the shetland pony.

right-about i.e. corrected.

"le type du voluptueux" i.e. the symbol of all that is voluptuous.

Chapter 20
The Concert

Mrs Bretton buys Lucy a pink dress for the concert at which royalty will be present. Lucy describes the journey through the streets of Villette, and, in some detail, the building they enter. On the way in Lucy sees herself in the mirror, and feels a jar of discord at the sight. Lucy observes one particular woman and describes her reactions. Dr John and his mother joke about her having a daughter-in-law. There follow the preparations for the entertainment with M.Paul's half-brother officiating, and M.Paul as usual well in evidence. The King, Queen and court of Labassecour then appear. Lucy studies the melancholy King, and is quite taken with the Queen despite her ancestry. In the assembled gathering Lucy sees some of her own pupils, and of course sees, and notes that Graham sees, Ginevra Fanshawe. Lucy gives some account of the concert. Afterwards she talks to Graham, who feels that Ginevra has been looking around and making fun of him and his mother. He reveals that he has seen into Ginevra and that she has broken his previous image of her. He is injured on his mother's account. When Graham talks to his mother, however, we realize that she too has noted Ginevra's behaviour but does not bother about it. M.Paul soon appears to help organize the lottery for the poor. The Queen speaks to Ginevra, but Graham, stifled by the heat, goes out with Lucy. He reiterates his new-found opinion of Ginevra. When they get back M.Paul looks closely at Lucy, but she keeps herself close to Graham's side. When Lucy looks at M.Paul she is aware that he is angry and mocking. Lucy and Graham each win a prize in the lottery; Graham further reveals that he has noticed the secret understanding between de Hamal and Ginevra. Graham has to take over the driving of the coach to get them home safely.

Commentary

This chapter focuses initially on Lucy's shyness, which is markedly noticeable over the dress. There is no doubt that she has an inferiority complex. But the occasion is a big one for her, and she describes it with her customary uncompromising independence, being particularly hard on the entertainers at the concert. What is interesting about this chapter is the effect of contrast which is achieved with most of the previous action – this is quite simply through the sense of public occasion as distinct from the sense of isolation, often desolation, experienced by Lucy. The major emphasis, though, is as always at this stage in the novel, on the reactions of Graham Bretton. His coming to terms with his own delusion is done very cleverly but very naturally – we know that he loves his mother, whose eccentricity is such that she is an easy prey for Ginevra's satire. Another interesting balance is that in Lucy's mind – she cannot ever overlook the presence of M.Paul, whose energy and rudeness fascinate her. This is a sign of the way her heart is moving, and there is a further interesting insight here since, with Graham seeing what she has wanted him to see in Ginevra, Lucy seems to be moving away from commitment to him herself. At this stage the movement is subconscious.

'au bénéfice des pauvres' On behalf of the poor.
lecture pieuse See note page 38.

the Slave of the Lamp Another *Arabian Nights* reference, here to Aladdin.

cupola The dome forming the roof of the building.

'giftie' 'the giftie gie us /To see oursels as others see us.' From *To a Mouse* by Robert Burns (1787).

Phidian From Phidias, fifth century BC Greek sculptor famous for his colossal statues in gold and ivory.

Juno In Roman mythology the Queen of the Roman Gods married to Jupiter.

like Jacob or Esau Genesis 28. Both Jacob and Esau were sent away to find wives, Jacob labouring for seven years for Leah, and then another seven for Rachel.

'reflets satinés Shining highlights.

'rose et blanches' 'Red and white.'

'The Vicar of Wakefield' The famous novel by Oliver Goldsmith (1730–74) which was published in 1764.

second déjeuner i.e. second lunch.

thereanent About that.

an ignorance crasse Complete ignorance.

'fausse' Fickle.

'au bénéfice des Pauvres' See note page 30.

Aphrodite In Greek mythology the goddess of love, identified with the Venus of Roman mythology.

paysanne Peasant.

just as Rhadamanthus One of three judges of the underworld in Greek mythology noted for his fairness.

'marchand de vin' Wine merchant.

Chapter 21
Reaction

Lucy eventually has to go back to the pensionnat. Graham sees her reluctance to return and promises he will write to her. Lucy debates with herself about whether this will happen, and then concludes that she must never reveal her feelings to him. Next day, a raw November one, she again thinks of life and its problems, particularly after her wrestling with Reason the previous night. When she looks up she finds that M. Paul is watching her; he sees that she is grieved at leaving the Brettons, and tries to engage her in conversation, but she refuses this. Reading quietly, Lucy is again interrupted, first by a polite pupil and then by Ginevra, who reveals how much she has enjoyed tormenting Graham. Lucy responds by giving her a false picture of Graham's reaction. A fortnight passes and Lucy finds that she is forgetting pain in 'the palsy of custom' (page 317). She sees Madame reading a letter, then has M.Paul burst in upon her, the latter to give her a letter from Graham Bretton. M.Paul is angry, Lucy goes away to conceal the letter so that she can read it later, and when she returns is verbally assaulted by M.Paul. He even assaults the stove, but is brought back to earth – and reason – when Lucy's voice falters. He lends her his handkerchief to wipe her eyes.

Commentary

Graham displays his customary considerateness. Lucy's reaction (from which the chapter receives its name) is a severe one, and she is thrown back upon herself, largely because she wishes to be. Ginevra is all selfish delight as tormentor, M.Paul in this chapter as mercurial as ever. Lucy's idea of repressing what she feels for Graham is expressed to herself after an intense inward debate, Reason as usual being personified. Madame Beck's surveillance, here through Rosine, is as stern as ever. Lucy has in fact returned to a kind of prison. M.Paul is obviously jealous at Lucy having the letter, takes it out on her and the class, but has the decency to see what he has done – injured Lucy – and to try to atone for it. It seems as if Lucy's reactions to him are an indicator of her depth of feeling, at this stage unknown to herself, for this strange and impassioned man who is extremely chauvinistic at one moment but kind and considerate at the next.

Nebo See Deuteronomy 34: 1–5 Moses sees the promised land from the top of the mountain.

'Mademoiselle, vous êtes triste' . . . **'Vous êtes . . . d'humeur.'** 'Miss you are sad.'

    'Sir, I have every right to be.'

    'You are sick in heart and disposition.'

'Que mademoiselle est appliquée!' 'How busy Miss is!'

'Pas de Géant' Giant step.

'Est-ce que vous avez . . .' 'Are you trying to insult me?'

'la jeunesse n'a qu'un temps' 'You're only young once.'

'Je conçois . . .' 'I understand, I understand – one understands the meaning of friend. Good-day miss.'

'Je vois bien que vous vous moquez . . .' 'I see only too well that you are laughing at me and my possessions.'

Chapter 22
The Letter

Lucy is striving hard to be alone so that she can read her letter, but she is initially thwarted. Eventually she gets some peace and reads Dr John's letter. But in the garret she thinks that she sees the legendary nun, gets down to Madame Beck's sitting-room, and urges the company to go up there. When they arrive to see if indeed there is anything wrong, Lucy finds that her letter has disappeared. She becomes somewhat distraught and is comforted by Dr John, who was among Madame Beck's company. Lucy cannot bring herself to tell him why it is that she cares so much for the letter. He then reveals that he has found it, and cross-questions her about what she has seen in the attic. He deduces that she is suffering badly from nerves. He urges her not to tell others of the matter and to try to be happy. He also tells her that he is free from his fascination with Ginevra. When he has gone Madame advises Lucy to say nothing to anyone.

Commentary

This chapter is rich in dramatic immediacy, with the delaying of Lucy's reading the letter a build up to the apparition of the nun. There is intense drama and subjectivity in Lucy's reaction to the situation, although she is calmed by the convenient and soothing presence of Dr John. Once more she is showing her dependence on him. Notice the Gothic atmosphere engendered by the description of the apparition as well as the now continuing discussion between Lucy and Dr John about his love for Ginevra being over. Both he and Madame are intent on urging Lucy to silence, and we can't help feeling that self-interest is involved in each case.

bougie Candle.
'Mais certainement ...' 'But certainly, precious, you can have two if you like.'
chiffonée i.e. dressed in chiffon.
doddered Old, unsteady.
grenier Attic.
the grovelling monomaniac Notice how Lucy gets outside herself and writes in the third person, as if she sees how others would see her at this moment.
'un air fin' A subtle air.

Happiness is not a potato ... There are times when Lucy is
refreshingly blunt, and this is one of them.

Chapter 23
Vashti

Lucy begins to believe in the prospect of happiness. The letters
she has had from Dr John have given her this confidence,
despite the objections from Reason. She goes out with the Brettons, and one evening Graham calls to take her to the theatre to
see one of the great actresses of the time. Lucy is so excited that
she has to bribe Rosine to help her dress. She gives a vivid
account of the performance and more particularly of the actress,
who she feels is possessed. She longs for Dr John's opinion, but
there follows the beginnings of what appears at the time to be a
serious fire. She and Graham help to extricate an Englishman
and his daughter from the chaos. The daughter gives Graham a
particularly penetrating look, and insists on thanking Lucy for
what she has done.

Commentary

Lucy is still well under the influence of Graham, her devotion to
the letters he has written her and the determination to court
happiness being evidence of this. Lucy's attitude towards the
actress underlines her puritanical streak. The fire, as a technical
device, serves two purposes: firstly it shows Dr John in his
customary good light in medical action; and secondly it helps the
plot forward by re-introducing a character vital to it. In case we
have not already identified her, her look at Graham is sufficient
indication. Thus the chapter closes on a dramatic note of expectation.

A new creed became mine ... Note that Lucy uses the spiritual, or
religious word, evidence of how strongly she feels.
Hebe In classical mythology, the daughter of Zeus. She filled the cups
of the gods, hence the reference here.
Reason ... Feeling Lucy frequently personifies her inward debates.
Rimmon See 2 Kings 5:1–18 for details of this double worship.
'On est là ...' 'There is someone to see you in the drawing-room.'
a day of Sirius Very hot (in reference to the dog-star).
neat-handed Phillis A direct quotation from Milton's *L'Allegro* 1.86.

a royal Vashti See Esther 1:1–22 for the story of King Ahasuerus. His beautiful wife refused to display herself to his court when he asked her to.

maenad Frenzied, in celebration of Bacchus, the God of wine in Greek mythology.

Saladin Probably the character of the Turk in Scott's *The Talisman* (1825).

Paul Peter Rubens (1577–1640), the celebrated Flemish painter.

a spirit out of Tophet The place of destruction in the valley of Ben – Hinnom. See 2 Kings 23:10.

Pythian inspiration Pythia was the priestess of Apollo at Delphi who delivered the oracles.

'I am not a child...' Pathetic, but this is how her father thinks of her, and it is going to make Graham Bretton's courtship difficult.

'prince Russe' Russian prince.

the serious, direct gaze ... peculiar in its gravity and intentness The clue that Paulina has recognized Dr John as the Graham Bretton of the past.

Chapter 24
M.de Bassompierre

Lucy is brooding on the fact that, after the memorable evening at the theatre, she hasn't heard from Dr John for seven weeks. She throws herself into various occupations in order to relieve the anxiety she feels. She re-reads the letters. One evening she is interrupted by Ginevra, who has been visiting her uncle de Bassompierre. Ginevra has been bored with the father and daughter, and reveals that Graham Bretton and his mother have been there too. Lucy longs for a letter from Graham but instead gets one from his mother, proposing to send a carriage for her on her half-holiday. Lucy ponders on the contrasting seven weeks which each of them has spent. Despite a snow-storm, Lucy pays the visit. When she arrives she finds Miss de Bassompierre there: the latter soon reveals that she is Paulina, and tells Lucy how attached she is to the past at Bretton. Lucy reminds her of Graham's attentions to her.

Commentary

Lucy is always a prey to nervous depression, as here. But she has a good sense of perspective, as she reveals when she gets Mrs Bretton's letter. We get the impression at this stage in the novel that the pensionnat is a prison for Lucy. Always solitary yet needing the affection of others, she nearly succumbs to that incipient melancholia again. The recognition of Paulina, like that of the Brettons earlier, strains the plot somewhat. Already we can see that the childhood scenes between Graham and Paulina are to be enacted, duplicated to a degree, at adult level. Lucy has no inkling of this at present, though she goes some way towards facilitating it by her reminders to Paulina of the past and of her (Paulina's) intimacy with Graham.

congeries Collection.
syne Since.
the Barmecide's loaf In one of *The Arabian Nights* the Barmecide puts an empty plate before his guest: the guest responds by pretending to enjoy the food. Barmecide's loaf = nothing.
Justement Certainly.
Esculapius i.e. the founder of medicine.
entrée i.e. free entrance to.
fuming in the vapours Sulking and collapsed in her frustration.
spun off the distaff i.e. completely gone.
coquelicot Poppy.
à l'endroit du gros Jean? about big John?
small-beer i.e. trivial, unimportant.
Nebuchadnezzar ... Chaldeans Daniel 4:7 His magicians, diviners, etc tried to interpret his dream, but only Daniel could do this.

Chapter 25
The Little Countess

The violent weather makes Mrs Bretton and Lucy worried about the safety of Graham and M.de Bassompierre. The latter is made much of by Paulina. The evening of celebration is described. Paulina casts herself in the role she used to have as a child with Graham. Lucy watches their confidences. The next day it is impossible to go out because of the weather. Paulina continues to recur to her childhood, particularly in her treatment of Graham. Paulina's father is seeking a school for her and questions Lucy; he also praises Lucy's independence. Graham notes some of Paulina's traits. When Graham and M.de Bassompierre go out, Paulina does not confide in Lucy: and when the two men return in the evening, no further contact is made between Lucy and Dr John.

Commentary

This revealing chapter gives us a keen insight into the character of Paulina, and we can certainly see that her interests are taken up with Dr John, and that the past is precious to her. Note her looking at the various volumes, and also the quietness which is expressive of real feeling (compare her behaviour with the superficiality of Ginevra Fanshawe). Paulina has charm and warmth, though we may find her a little cloying in her attitude towards her father, whom she tries to cosset, just as she did when she was a child. In fact, to coin Wordsworth's phrase, the child is mother of the woman – Paulina has recognizably developed from what she was. There is interesting narrative speculation about Lucy's own views of what is happening under her eyes.

that mask of old Christmas The two men look like Twelfth Night celebrators, the date of Old Christmas.
pas de fée, ou de fantaisie Neither fairy or fantasy.
curious Well-brewed.
'pistolets' Rolls.
'too – too solid flesh' 'O that this too, too solid flesh would melt' (*Hamlet* Act I Scene 2), one of his major soliloquies.

Chapter 26
A Burial

Madame Beck approves of Lucy's social connections, but abstracts the five letters from Dr John, returning them later. Lucy decides to get rid of them, misses them again from their place, and then realizes that Madame is confiding in M.Paul. This determines her upon immediate action. She has the letters sealed in a bottle, and hides them in the old pear-tree. Afterwards she sees a 'tall, sable-robed, snowy-veiled woman' (page 381). Later Paulina asks her to become her companion, but Lucy values her independence too much to do so. Madame Beck, though spying on her, also leaves her some independence which she values. Lucy observes Mary (as she calls Paulina) and notes how she pleases her father with her politeness to Dr John. Lucy also observes that M.De Bassompierre seems blind to what is happening. Lucy likes him, and comes to appreciate Paulina as they study together. M.Paul begins to be obtrusive again. Lucy and Paulina read Schiller together, and Lucy is critical of

Ginevra, who has of course been satirical about Graham and his mother. There is to be a dinner the next day, and Ginevra will be invited.

Commentary

Lucy shows that she, at least, knows what is happening between Graham and Paulina – hence her desire to get rid of the letters. There is more spying (Madame inevitably); there is more Gothic atmosphere (the encounter with the 'nun'); there is the developing relationship between Paulina and Graham. Paulina, childlike in some ways, gives the impression of being determined too. It is also apparent that she is jealous of Ginevra, and feels that the latter is playing about with Graham. In discussing this, and love after reading the Schiller lyrics, she reveals the state of her own heart to Lucy.

grade i.e. status.
'Oui, oui . . . louable.' Yes, yes my good friend, I freely give you permission from my heart. Your work in my house has always been good, zealous and full of discretion. You have every right to amuse yourself. Go out whenever you like. As to your choice of companions, I am happy with it. It is wise, dignified and worthy of praise.'
the valley of Sinbad From *The Arabian Nights*, where Sinbad discovers the diamond valley on one of his voyages.
'Il y a . . . Anglais' 'There is something very remarkable in the character of the English.'
'Je ne saurais . . . de les surveiller' 'I don't quite know how to explain it, but briefly the English have their own ideas on friendship, love, indeed everything. But at least there is no need to keep your eye on them.'
Ichabod See 1 Samuel 4. Ichabod means 'no glory' and is synonymous with an expression of regret.
Overcast enough it was my nature often to be . . . An important indicator of Lucy's character.
'c'est ce que je ferai' 'That is what I will do'.
méchant Naughty.
callant Young man.
learned and blue i.e. a blue-stocking, a learned woman.
"en l'air" In the air.
"religièuses" Saints.
'dévouement' Devotion.
'récueillement' Contemplativeness.
'Sacré' Sacred.
mille Thousand.

Deutsch German.
Undine Female water-sprite.
Schiller's Ballads Schiller, German dramatist and poet (1759–1805).
'Des Mädchens Klage' The Maiden's Lament.
'Du Heilige . . .' 'You holy one, summon your child back, I have
  enjoyed earthly pleasure, I have lived and loved!'
savants i.e. learned people.

Chapter 27
The Hôtel Crécy

Lucy is to attend a discourse by one of the Professors in honour
of the prince's birthday. Meanwhile, she talks to Ginevra, who is
rather surprised at their apparent equality of status. They go to
the Hôtel Crécy, then to the assembly. Lucy finds that M.Paul is
to give the address, which proves to be a politically inspiring one.
He sees Lucy when she leaves, and is invited back to the Crécy.
At dinner (M.Paul is to come on later) Lucy watches Paulina,
whose French is very good, Graham and Ginevra. The latter is
animated only when there are men present, but it is Paulina who
gets most of the male attention. M.Paul arrives but holds back
when he sees that Lucy is in the company of Graham. The latter
carries on a bantering conversation with Lucy, who becomes
annoyed by some of the phrases Graham uses about Ginevra.
Graham reveals that he was aware that Paulina was fond of him
in the past. As Graham asks Lucy to content him, M.Paul makes
an insulting comment to Lucy. But Graham leaves Lucy's side to
talk to Paulina, and M.Paul tries to find out what he can about
Lucy's feelings. He apologizes for his earlier words. Lucy goes
home with Ginevra, and again puts Ginevra in her place.

Commentary

This is a public chapter – Lucy, and the others, are on show
because of the occasion. Ginevra is as facile and superficial as
ever, constantly flirting, though Lucy pays tribute to her direct-
ness. There is a degree of narrative tension aroused on two
distinct counts – the first is the quality of the discourse given by
M.Paul, and Lucy's obvious interest in it. This shows the way her
own feelings are developing. The second is the contrast between
Paulina and Ginevra, a contrast which Graham cannot fail to
notice. What he does fail to do, however, is to realize that Lucy

can be easily hurt by his innuendo. Lucy's own feelings seem to be at full stretch in this chapter, for she has to cope with the ebullient M.Paul as well. We feel after her exchange with him that, having been trapped emotionally by the two men in whom she is interested, Lucy takes out her frustrations on Ginevra. This reaction is both excusable and justifiable.

bourgmestre Burgomaster.
regnant ... estrade Ruling on his raised platform.
'Qu'en dîtes vous?' 'What did you think of it?'
Nero The cruel and tyrannical Roman Emperor (37–68 AD).
Petite chatte ... je dois l'avoir!' 'You provocative little coquette ... you seem to be sad, timid, dreamy, but you aren't. I'm telling you that. Savage! With a flaming soul and that light in your eyes!'
'Yes, I do have a blazing soul and I have the right to have one.'
ce grand fat That big fop.
'Mon ami, je vous pardonne.' 'My friend, I forgive you.'
Bon ... Volià que le jour ... 'Good ... Look how the dawn is breaking. Speak thus, my friend.'
a John Knox to a Mary Stuart Heavy irony – John Knox (1505–72) the Scottish religious reformer and Mary Queen of Scots, Catholic born 1542, executed 1587. Knox, strongly anti-Catholic, was uncompromising in his attacks on her.

Revision questions on Chapters 16–27 (Volume Two)

1 What do you find melodramatic or unconvincing about any of these chapters? Refer to the text in some detail in support of your views.

2 Compare and contrast Graham Bretton and M.Paul as they appear in Volume II.

3 Indicate, as directly as possible, how far the past influences the present in any two of the characters (including Lucy).

4 Write an account of the most exciting incident in these chapters.

5 Say what you find attractive about *two* of the following (a) Mrs Bretton: (b) M.de Bassompierre: (c) Paulina Mary.

6 How far do you sympathize with Lucy in her relationships with Graham and M.Paul? You should refer closely to the text in your answer.

7 'Lucy is thoroughly neurotic.' How far do you think that this is a fair assessment?

Volume Three
Chapter 28
The Watchguard

The chapter opens with an account of the aggressive nature of M.Paul in class and his intolerance of interruptions. Rosine being afraid to brave him again, Lucy herself goes to bear M.Paul a message. He eventually condescends to allow her to deliver it, but says he will not go. Lucy urges him in her own way, and in doing so breaks his glasses. His reaction is more saintly than annoyed, much to her surprise. Later that evening they do quarrel though, when he interrupts the hour of study and reads dramatically from a bad translation of Shakespeare. He accosts Lucy, who tells him that she is making a watchguard. He also accuses her of dressing ostentatiously. Lucy realizes that she does not appear to him as she appears to others, or even to herself.

Commentary

The focus in this chapter is almost exclusively on Lucy and M.Paul. That focus underlines their gradual movement towards each other. M.Paul reveals a much greater degree of tolerance and sympathetic warmth than we might have expected. Lucy shows her usual courage when she is pushed to an extremity. In a word, M.Paul is exhibiting all the signs of jealousy. Lucy has plenty of time to ponder on his accusations which not only show his demonstrative and domineering nature but also his capacity to endure a range of feelings.

momently i.e. with each increasing moment.
'Mon Dieu' ... d'une colère!' My God! my God! What will become of me? I'm sure that Monsieur is going to kill me, he is in such a rage!'
'Dès ce moment' ... 'From this moment – the classroom is banned. The first person to open the door, or to pass through that division, will be hanged – even should it be Madame Beck herself!'
'Ouf! Je n'en puis plus!' 'I can no longer do it!'
lunettes Glasses.
'Que me voulez-vous?' 'What do you want with me?'

'**je veux l'impossible . . .**' 'I want what is impossible, unheard of things.'

'**Là! . . . me voilà . . .**' 'Here I am deprived of my glasses.'

'**une forte femme . . .**' An overpowering woman, a virago.

bonnet-grec i.e. Greek hat.

à l'improviste On the spur of the moment.

feuilleton Leaflet = newspaper.

silent as nuns in a'retreat' An unobtrusive echo of what is a mystery in *Villette*.

tropics i.e. circles.

'**Ne bougez pas**' 'Don't move.'

I wish you were at Jericho 2 Samuel 10:4–5. David's servants were told to wait at Jericho until their beards grew again. The phrase means 'well away from me.'

'**Vous ne voulez pas . . . mesdemoiselles**' 'You don't want me for a neighbour – you give yourself airs of superiority: you treat me as an outcast. Right! I'm going to settle this. Ladies, you are all to stand up!'

'**Est ce assez . . . la main**' 'Is that a good enough distance?'
  'Monsieur is the best judge of that.'
  'You know that's not true. It is you who have made this deep division. It is not of my making.'

'**un drame . . . de ces sots paiens**' 'A play by Shakespeare, the false god of these foolish pagans, the English.'

caractére intraitable Obstinate nature.

fougue Fire.

Chut' . . . ou moins bien fait' Silence this minute . . . quick to flare up . . . anger . . . heat . . . doll-like colours . . . a tolerably well-formed nose.

'**des cols brodés**' 'Embroidered collars.'

'**colfichet de plus**' 'One more bauble.'

'**babioles**' knick-knacks.

des façons mondaines' Society fashions.

'**bure**' . . . '**gris de poussière**' Homespun . . . dusty grey.

Va pour le ruban! (The ribbon) is suitable.

Chapter 29
Monsieur's Fête

Lucy's conscientiousness is evident in her preparations. The tributes to M.Paul are many, with Zélie St Pierre leading the way in a flirtatious manner. Lucy, unlike all the others, has no bouquet. M.Paul appears to be in a very good mood, and has dressed for the occasion. Three times after the presentations he asks if that is all, obviously hurt by the fact that Lucy has given him nothing. Zélie tells him that Lucy has thought the ceremony too frivolous to demand her attention. He launches an attack upon England and the English, and Lucy is moved to answer back. Later, when Lucy goes to her room she finds M.Paul going through her desk. He has left her gifts of books and magazines in the past, so that she is aware of his habit. He has bought her two books as a token of his forgiveness of the morning's actions on her part. He taxes her somewhat, but she shows that she does know the correct observance required by giving him the watchguard with its initials. In the evening Lucy feels that he is very friendly towards her.

Commentary

The coming-together process continues. We feel for Lucy as everyone else presents a bouquet. Zélie shows her spitefulness, M.Paul his usual inability to do things without moderation – he is either benevolence or anger personified. We feel that although he goes to Lucy's desk and leaves things for her, he is also perhaps checking up on behalf of Madame Beck or, more assuredly, himself, since he is jealous of Lucy's friendships. But he endears himself to us by his warm and artless approval of the present she made him.

'robe de soie' Silk dress.
'gôuter un peu les plaisirs' To taste a little pleasure.
'Est-ce là tout?' 'Is that all?' It is reiterated, for M.Paul is certainly looking for something from Lucy.
'mappe-monde' Map of the world.
'Vive l'Angleterre . . . Long Live England, History and Heroes. Down with France, its Fiction and its Fops!'
'Donc je n'y . . . Soit!' 'Then I shall not be there.'
    'So be it!'
brownie Benevolent shaggy goblin.
untimely churn See note in Penguin edition page 615.
'je te déteste . . .' 'I hate you, my boy!'
'Dieu vous en garde!' 'God save you from it!'
bonbonnière Sweet-box.
dragées Sweet.
brioche Bun.
'À présent c'est un fait accompli' 'At present it's an accomplished fact'.

Chapter 30
M.Paul

Lucy compares the moodiness and the extremes of behaviour of M.Paul to those of the Emperor Napoleon. The episode with Madame Panache and its aftermath is given as a particular example. M.Paul is an exacting taskmaster and takes Lucy in hand over her arithmetic. There are the usual rows and rejections, but Lucy finds that the books she put away from her are restored by M.Paul. The latter reacts in his usual way when Lucy is summoned to go to a lecture by Dr John. There are further exchanges as M.Paul suspects that Lucy is adept in the classical languages. But, as she puts it, 'his bark was worse than his bite' (page 443). M.Paul wants Lucy to improvise a composition in French. This is their battleground. She esapes from his houndings.

Commentary

This is an exploration of a developing relationship which is based on conflict. Lucy feels a strong sense of imprisonment and has the strength and independence to liberate herself from it at times. But we must allow that there is a tendency towards masochism in Lucy's character, and in a sense she enjoys the trials and tribulations she suffers at M.Paul's hands, for there is always the swing to the other side – his kindness, his simple generosity, his sharing. Each is fighting not to be subdued: but the mere fact that they are in each other's company so much means that they are assuredly coming together.

Madame de Staels Madame de Stael was the French authoress (1766–1817) who established a progressive and revolutionary salon.
strange taking i.e. mood.
Penthesilea A queen of the Amazons.
charity-schoolboy i.e. schools set up for the poor. They provided only minimal education.
Eutychus Acts 20,:9–12. He was presumed dead, but later found to be merely in a deep sleep.
'Qu'il est vraiment beau' . . . 'sans pudeur.' 'How truly handsome is this young doctor. What eyes – what a look! See! My heart is overcome! . . .' 'that brazen girl . . . that creature without any modesty.
'Elle ne dit . . . sans doute' 'She only speaks the truth.'
     Ah. You believe that.'

'Yes, certainly.'

the flowers of Hymettus The range of hills near Athens known for their beautiful flowers.

'Cela ne me regarde pas . . .' 'That doesn't concern me. I couldn't care less about it.'

'Petite gourmande!' Little glutton!

mere sound and fury, signifying nothing *Macbeth* Act 5 Scene 5 just after the death of Lady Macbeth. This is part of Macbeth's famous soliloquy.

indurated Made hard.

Baal The god of the ancient Phoenicians and Canaanites. False god, idol.

Dagon The fertility God, supposedly the father of Baal.

vatication Prophecy.

'orgueil de diable' Pride of the devil.

'je vous vois d'ici' 'I can see you from here.'

Chapter 31
The Dryad

On a spring afternoon Lucy goes for a walk, returns, and watches Madame Beck's guests and, more particularly, M.Paul and his god-daughter. Lucy falls asleep, and finds that she has been taken care of when she awakes. Later Lucy walks in her favourite spot and ponders on life and whether she should set up a school on her own. While she is leaning against Methusalah, and thinking of the packet of Dr John's letters she has hidden there, she speaks aloud to him, but finds that she is in the presence of M.Paul. He tells her of his observation post over the garden. He manages to convince her that there is some affinity between them despite the differences in their natures and tells Lucy that he has sometimes seen the nun. There is a noise in the great tree, and they both see the figure of the nun rush past them.

Commentary

There are indications here that once more Lucy is tiring herself out, and also that she is already a little possessive over M.Paul, as she watches the god-daughter. This almost anticipates her feelings over his devotion to his dead 'spiritual' love Justine. We see her fear of herself and her involvement with M.Paul in her pondering on a future away from him. Lucy's words, and the symbolism of the tree, connect the past with the present. M.Paul's spying shows his own arrogance of nature, while Lucy's response shows her own moral standards. The Gothic manifestation of the nun means that the chapter ends on a note of mystery.

The Dryad Tree-nymph in classical mythology.
'cette maîtresse-femme' i.e. this formidable woman.
'Comment?' How?
Calvin or Luther The great protestants, the first the French theologian (1509–64), the second the leader of the Protestant reformation in Germany (1483–1546).
patte de velours Velvet paw.

Chapter 32
The First Letter

One afternoon in April Lucy sees the Bassompierres and Graham Bretton. The following evening she sees Paulina, who is obviously still concerned about Graham's interest in Ginevra. Paulina wants to confide in Lucy, and does so. First of all she questions her about Graham's character, then reveals that Graham has written to her: a letter telling of his love for her. She is anxious about telling her father, but Lucy gives her good advice: M.de Bassompierres has got to learn that his daughter has grown up.

Commentary

This chapter is made exquisite by the sensitivity Paulina shows in her love for Graham and her concern for her father. This is complemented by Lucy's concern for Paulina and her happiness. There is too the realism with which she appraises Graham's character: while allowing all his good points she sees that it is essential to him to have a wife in a position of social status. Paulina is very much the child she was, but there is a warmth about her nature which is endearing.

victrix Victorious woman.

Chapter 33
M.Paul Keeps His Promise

This chapter describes the breakfast in the country: Ginevra gets on M.Paul's nerves and he criticizes, by implication, what Lucy is wearing. M.Paul charms Lucy and the company with the quality of the story he tells them. They breakfast at the farm, with M.Paul as usual organizing everything. Lucy notices that M.Paul says a prayer, and although he considers her an infidel, he holds out the hand of friendship to her again. He hints to Lucy that he may go away, and asks her how she would do without him. When they get back she sees him talking to Madame Beck. There is obviously something on M.Paul's mind. He strides towards where Lucy is, but she flees, only to hear Zélie say that she has gone to bed. Madame Beck seizes M.Paul and conveys him outside.

Commentary

The idyll of the country trip shows M.Paul in good form and Lucy becoming more and more enamoured of him. There is certainly something worrying him. Lucy, however, is concerned to explain the stimulus she gets from his mind. The spitefulness of Zélie is characteristic, and Lucy takes her sufferings to bed with her.

'Je vous conseille . . .' 'I advise you to give yourself an invitation.'
in excellent case i.e. in strong fashion.
'Qu'est ce que c'est? . . .' 'What is it? Are you playing jokes on me?'
'c'est la robe rose!' It is the pink dress!'
'Et Mademoiselle Lucie . . .' 'And Miss Lucy is as much of a coquette as ten Parisiennes. Have you ever seen anyone to equal this Englishwoman. Just look at her hat, her gloves and her boots!'
'Courage! – à vrai dire . . . la propreté' To speak the truth, I am not annoyed, perhaps I am somewhat happy that a person has made herself so pretty for my little fête.'
   'But my dress isn't pretty, monsieur, it is only suitable.'
   'I like such suitability.'
'les bois et les petits sentiers' 'The woods and the little paths'.
collyrium Eye lotion.
fermière . . . café au lait Farmer's wife . . . coffee.
jambon . . . 'confitures' . . . 'des ménagères avares' Ham . . . jams . . . mean housekeepers.
'Donnez moi la main!' 'Give me your hand!'

Corneille Pierre Corneille, French classical dramatist (1606–84).
'Petite soeur' 'Little sister'.
'Pourtant, j'ai été . . . However, I have been very hard, very stern with you.
'Où est Mademoiselle Lucie?' 'Where is Miss Lucy?'
'Elle est au lit' 'She is in bed.'

Chapter 34
Malevola

Lucy is sent into town by Madame Beck to see Madame Wal-ravens. She also does some shopping for Madame. As she reaches the house she sees an old priest leaving it. He comes back and helps Lucy gain admittance to the house. After being left in a salon, Lucy is approached by an old, deformed woman who rejects her offerings and the message from Madame Beck. Later Lucy is joined by the old priest, who turns out to be Père Silas. He tells her the story of Justine Marie's death and of M.Paul's devotion to her memory. We also learn where M.Paul's money goes and why he is so poor. When she gets back Lucy reports to Madame Beck, who gives her own version of the story which confirms the debts, the burden of providing, which M.Paul has.

Commentary

This chapter is a plot chapter, this is to say, it exists to bring Lucy into a state of knowledge with regard to M.Paul as she is falling in love with him. There is an element of the Gothic and the grotesque in this chapter. The revelations about M.Paul pressur-ize Lucy, since they show just how devoted to his religion he is, and just how unlikely to love in the present in view of his loyalty to the memory of Justine Marie. We get the impression that the journey and the reception, together with the convenient appear-ance of Père Silas and his telling Lucy the story, are quite deliberate: Lucy has been 'set-up' in an attempt to put her off M.Paul.

cabas Bonnet.
tripotage Awkward business.
Tadmor 2 Chronicles 8:4 Solomon rebuilt Tadmore in the wilderness.

'Que me voulez-vous?' 'What do you want with me?'

et quant à ses félicitations ... And as for her greetings, I have no interest in them.

Sidonia The Jewish character in Disraeli's novel *Coningsby*.

like a prayer of litany Père Silas is reading his breviary.

Rousseau-like sentimentalizing From Jean Jacques Rousseau (1712–78), French philosopher who believed in a return to the natural state in which man is both good and happy.

the Bourse The money market, the Paris equivalent of the Stock Exchange.

'Donc ... donc, vous devez ...' 'Well ... well, then you must know my pupil, my Paul?

'pax vobiscum' 'Peace be with you.'

'Elle est drôle ... She is funny (odd), isn't she?

'Oh la singulière petite bossue! ...' 'Oh, the odd little hunchback! And do you know that she hates me, because she thinks that I am in love with my cousin Paul? That pious little man who dare not move unless his confessor has given him permission to. However ... whether it were me, or another.'

'personnage assez niaise ...' Someone who seems to me to be silly enough.

'pure comme un lis' As pure as a lily, according to him.

'oubliez les anges ...' Forget the angels, the hunchbacks and, above all, the professors – and good night!'

Chapter 35
Fraternity

Lucy emphasizes that in being told to forget she remembers the more. M.Paul has become even more humanized for her. Lucy is not frightened – she knows that M.Paul would have done just the same by anybody else as he has done to Justine Marie. The next day she is hurried before two professors who have come to examine her in order to prove that she wrote her own work and not M.Paul. They are silly enough to set Lucy an essay on Human Justice. Lucy writes the essay from her own highly individualistic, independent and satirical standpoint. Afterwards Lucy talks with M.Paul about himself, and reveals to him that she knows of his responsibilities. She tells him his own story, which she has but lately learned. He asks her to be his sister: Lucy is flattered and deeply moved by this; and he tells her not to think of the vision of the nun.

Commentary

The dramatic interview with the two professors has some comic elements in it. It is a vehicle for getting Lucy into a rebellious state of mind. It shows how impetuous and undisciplined M.Paul can be on occasions. There is no doubt that he is touched by what Lucy tells him she now knows. In fact, he is vulnerable on this count and also about his professional ability – this is really why Lucy is put to the test – to stop his professional pride from being undermined. Nevertheless there are indications that he is greatly moved by Lucy and that his committing himself in this way is a token of the greater commitment he feels – love – but which he cannot give himself to.

adytum Innermost part, private chamber.
in *propria persona* In her own role.
Grand Ciel! Good Heavens!
Boissec and Rochemorte Drywood and Deadrock, sufficient indication of their function here.
Mérovée from Pharamond Two legendary heroes of the Franks in the 5th century AD.
'Je n'en sais rien' 'I don't know anything about it.'
'Est-elle donc idiote?' 'Is she a complete idiot?'
'Nous agissons dans l'intêret . . .' 'We are acting in the interests of truth. We don't want to injure you.'
Saul . . . Joab See I Samuel 18 and 19 for the source of Saul's sadness. Joab was the warrior in command of David's army.
a crow to pluck with him A phrase which means having to settle or resolve something.
'une petite moqueuse . . .' 'A little mocker without a heart.'
'Et vous, mademoiselle . . .' 'And you Miss; you are neat and tender, and completely hard-hearted into the bargain.'
'Je vis dans un trou!' 'I live in a hole!'
'Je fais mon lit . . .' 'I make my bed and clean my house.'
boudoir-oratoire The bedroom-oratory.
'Et puis?' 'And then?'
'n'est il pas vrai?' Isn't it true?

Chapter 36
The Apple of Discord

The next day Lucy has difficulty in making contact with M.Paul. In the evening she waits for her lesson with M.Paul. The latter is occupied with his spaniel Sylvie and does not come to teach her as he should have done. When Lucy goes to her desk she finds a Roman Catholic tract in it. She concludes that M.Paul has been to see Père Silas, and that the latter has urged him to try to convert Lucy. After Sylvie has disturbed the books and papers, M.Paul asks Lucy if she has read the brochure which he left for her; when further questioned Lucy says she was unmoved by it. He tells her that he hardly knows what he thinks of her, but that his friends have counselled caution. He puts her through a course of Catholic reasoning aided by Père Silas, who prescribes her reading. She is taken to churches but cannot respond to the faith: she rebels, but M.Paul knows that she has a sincere faith of her own, and asks God to bless her.

Commentary

The main emphasis in this chapter is on the attempts to convert Lucy, but she remains as adamantly anti-Catholic as ever. Behind these attempts is M.Paul's own piety and his as yet unacknowledged love for Lucy. If she can be won to his religion then they will be free to love each other. If she cannot? The narrative hinges on her resistance – but the relationship that she has with M.Paul is built on conflict and resolution. His tender-ness at the end of the chapter speaks volumes about the state of his heart.

'Petite exigeante!' 'Demanding little creature!'
ennuis Apathy.
St Vincent de Paul The French priest who founded a hospice for orphans, founder also of a missionary society and of the Sisters of Charity (1576–1660).
the ruddy old lady of the Seven Hills Rome.
'more honoured in the breach than in the observance' See *Hamlet* I:4 line 16.
'trop de sensibilité and de sympathie' too much sensibility and sympathy.'
'Dites-donc, petite soeur' Tell me then, little sister.
'Oh, cela me fait mal!' 'Oh, that makes me feel bad!'
'Marie, Reine du Ciel' 'Mary, Queen of Heaven.'
Moloch The Canaanite God to whom child-sacrifices were made.
her whose painted and meretricious face i.e. The Roman Catholic Church, the language sufficiently indicative of Lucy's strength of feeling.
'O Dieu, sois appaisé . . .' 'O God, forgive me who am a sinner'.

Chapter 37
Sunshine

Lucy contemplates the growing together of Paulina and Graham Bretton: Graham in fact improves in his cultural associations, while Lucy as ever continues as confidante to Paulina. The father also talks to Lucy about the matter; he is obviously upset, and feels that Dr John is not good enough for his daughter. Father and daughter talk somewhat uneasily about Graham, and Lucy goes out to meet the latter when he arrives. Graham is of course apprehensive, but Lucy is confident of his success. The engagement is grudgingly allowed by M.de Bassompierre, although when Lucy sees the three of them later she knows that Paulina has succeeded in binding the two men together.

Commentary

This is the working out of the sub-plot involving Paulina and Graham. In the course of it M.De Bassompierre becomes something of a caricature possessive father, over-reacting, until he gruffly concedes. For Lucy it is a chapter of sympathetic reportage, a lull in her own affairs, it takes her outside herself. Since Paulina is so good, we feel a drop in narrative interest.

demeaned herself i.e. carried or conducted herself.
'pétrie d'esprit...' 'Shaped of wit and graces'.
pot-hooks Writing like the curved hooks with which lids were lifted off pots.
"braw wooer" Brave wooer.
Pentelicus A mountain having marble quarries near Athens.
Rachel weeping for her children Jeremiah 31:15 Herod had ordered the slaughter of boy children under two in Bethlehem.

Chapter 38
Cloud

Madame Beck announces that M.Paul is leaving. Lucy rallies, but is very upset, as are many of the girls. She overhears Madame Beck talking to Zélie about M.Paul's duty calling him to the West Indies. A week passes, and Lucy thinks back to the time when she and M.Paul had been interrupted by Madame Beck and Père Silas. Shortly after that M.Paul's departure has been announced. The last day arrives, and still no sign of M.Paul, until he comes and takes his leave of the girls, while Lucy is kept occupied by Madame Beck, and he does not see Lucy to say goodbye. He sends her a note, however, telling her to be ready to see him. She stays up that night, and is reprimanded by Madame. In a flash of intuition Lucy feels that Madame wishes to marry Paul herself. She struggles through the next day and is given an opiate that night. She reacts against it, gets up and makes for the main park. She sees the Bassompierre carriage pass her, and soon finds herself in the middle of a night fête. She is helped by the bookseller Miret, and observes the Bassompierres. After that she sees a little girl, realizes that it is Madame Beck's daughter Désirée, and then sees Madame Beck and the rest of what she calls 'the whole conjuration, the secret junta' (page 558).

Commentary

This is a highly dramatic sequence throughout. Lucy is intensely subjective about the news, as we should expect her to be. We feel that the plot to remove M.Paul has now taken full effect, and that he is being urged to go away in order to stop him marrying Lucy. Such is Lucy's state of mind that she immediately jumps to the conclusion that it is Madame Beck who is her rival. The night trip to the park presents us with a series of scenes. We have to suspend our disbelief, as it is quite incredible that, apart from being seen by the bookseller Lucy should escape recognition. The effect is to make the scene melodramatic as it is difficult to accept it as realism. In fact there is a dreamlike quality about the whole sequence.

His will be done A deliberate echo of The Lord's Prayer.
an Alnaschar dream i.e. one that will not be realized. From the character in *The Arabian Nights* who smashed all his glassware and was therefore unable to realize a profit by selling it.
'Il est doux, le repos! . . .' It is sweet to have rest. It is precious to have tranquil happiness.
'Bonne petite amie! . . .' My little friend . . . sweet consoler.
a Jean-Jacques sensibility See note page 70 for the 'innocence' of Rousseau.
Apollyon . . . Greatheart Evil and good characters respectively in John Bunyan's *The Pilgrim's Progress* (1678).

dévot Fanatic (in the religious sense).
'Que vous êtes pâles!' 'How pale you are! You are very ill, then, Miss!'
chou-chou Sweetly, peacefully.
flambeaux Lights.
Peri-Banou Another *Arabian Nights* reference.
ébats Frolics.

Chapter 39
Old and New Acquaintance

Lucy now tells us what she has been able to pick up about the situation in the past few weeks. Madame Walravens is rich, with an estate in Guadaloupe, and Madame Beck, a distant relative, has been courting her for her money. M.Paul has been pressurized to go out to Guadaloupe as steward of the estates. At this stage Lucy still thinks M.Paul has gone abroad. She hears talk of 'Justine Marie', sees a pretty Belgian girl, and then realizes that it is the god-daughter of M.Paul. Lucy then realizes M.Paul is also present. The part-explanation is over, but this is not the haunting nun of the garden. It seems likely, though a young German is present, that M.Paul has been promised this young girl on his return. Convinced by what she has seen, Lucy now determines to go home. As she does so a white handkerchief flutters from a window of a carriage. When she gets to the dormitory she finds the effigy of the nun on her bed, with a note to say that she will bother Lucy no more.

Commentary

Again the dramatic element is present throughout as Lucy views the assembly and draws her own conclusions. We must remember that her state is heightened by the drug, and that her imagination is working overtime. In fact the plot is being unravelled at great speed, with the white handkerchief and the 'nun's' note contributing to the Gothic atmosphere. Lucy, as always in times of crisis, conducts an inward debate with herself.

its Alpha is Mammon, and its omega, Interest The beginning and end of it all is greed and selfishness.
'Où sont-ils?...' 'Where are they? Why don't they come?'
Witch-of-Endor See Samuel I 28:7 The sorceress was consulted by Saul before the battle of Gilboa.
'Là voilà!... Look there!... here's Justine Marie coming!'

'Paul et Virginie' Bernardin de St Pierre's sentimental story (1787).
'la petite va m'aider...' 'The little one is going to help—isn't that so?'
'Mais oui, je vous aiderai...' 'But yes, I will help you with all my heart.
 You can do with me whatever you wish, godfather.'
'nuit blanche' White night, indicating that it is all lit up.

Chapter 40
The Happy Pair

The next day, a fine summer's one, Ginevra Fanshawe has disappeared. Ginevra reveals in a letter that de Hamal was 'the nun of the attic' (page 573) and the several incidents involving him are referred to. Ginevra has married him, having achieved what she wanted, namely the status of a countess. Later she goes abroad with him, and dotes on her child, but gets into debt and turns to M.de Bassompierre for help and sympathy.

Commentary

This is a rounding off of the nun incidents. Ginevra's selfishness is as ever apparent, and Lucy is unsparing in her ironic appraisal too. De Hamal is exactly what we should expect. We get the impression of irresponsibility being carried forward into married life, and we are obviously being invited to make comparisons with the love of Paulina and Graham and, even more strongly, the conflict that leads to passionate love as in the case of Lucy and M.Paul.

En revanche In return.
'détournement de mineur' Abducting a minor.
'in articulo mortis' On the point of death.

Chapter 41
Faubourg Clotilde

Despite all her reasoning, Lucy is again in a state of tension. M.Paul puts her out of her misery by appearing. Madame Beck summons him away from Lucy, but when Lucy says that her heart will break, M.Paul refuses to leave her. Madame Beck brings all that she can to bear upon him, but he raises his hand to her and she flees. M.Paul tells Lucy that he has come to justify himself. He has come to take her into town. On the way Lucy's feelings become clear to herself and to him, and his to her. He will be away for three years. Lucy gets him to promise to write to her. After that he takes her to the school that is to be hers, and tells her of the arrangements he has made. This is what he has spent his time doing. He explains about Justine Marie, and he says to Lucy – 'take my love. One day share my life, be my dearest, first on earth.' (page 591). The next day he leaves on his voyage.

Commentary

This is the consummation chapter in the sense that Lucy and M.Paul understand each other and, despite his conditioning at the hands of Madame Beck, he proves that he is his own man – and Lucy's. His secret with Lucy shows his own nature to be true despite the pressures which have been laid upon him. At the same time we feel that the provision of the school is perhaps too much – it ties Lucy to him because he has done this. It is almost an investment in his future if he wants a future with her.

'ouvrier' Workman.
'Laissez-moi! . . . .' 'Sortex d'ici!. . . .' 'Femme!. . .' 'Leave me . . .' 'Go from here . . .' 'Leave at once!'
'Elle est toute pâle . . .' 'She is completely pallid – that face makes me feel ill.'
'Doucement . . . soyez tranquille.' Gently, gently – be calm.
'Externat de demoiselles . . . Directrice' Day-school for young ladies . . . Headmistress'.
Polichinelle! Punch!

Chapter 42
Finis

This is exactly what it says it is, and requires no division of summary and commentary. The idea of Lucy and M.Paul being happy after years of separation – what Lucy herself calls a paradox – is true because Lucy has always obeyed a work-ethic by which she lives. This is the nature of her fulfilment. There are also the letters she receives from M.Paul. These enable her to be successful because of the emotional sustenance with which they provide her. There is more than that. They provide enlightenment too, for in his newly found tolerance M.Paul insists that Lucy continue to be a Protestant. In a man of more phlegmatic nature this would be condescension: in M.Paul it is a reflex and a reflection of his love. The 'puzzle' which marks the end of the novel is typical of the high ambiguity of Charlotte Brontë's art. Does M.Paul die in the storms? Does he die in Lucy's dreams in the storms? Or does he survive it all and return to her? Such has been the uncertainty of Lucy's life and the neurosis of her obsessions and beliefs that the ambiguity puts the final seal on her 'autobiography' amost as if, in the last instance, she is taking some delight in teasing the reader.

Juggernaut The idol of Krishna under whose chariot wheels the devoted worshippers throw themselves.
craunch Dialect for crunch.
Banshee The spirit which wails under the windows of a house where one of those inside is about to die.
Let them picture union and a happy succeeding life i.e. the traditional happy ending for those who want it.

Revision questions in Chapters 28—42 Volume Three

1 By close reference to the text, show how Lucy's love for M.Paul increases during these chapters.

2 Write an account of the circumstances which lead to the coming together of Paulina and Graham Bretton.

3 Which do you consider to be the most dramatic event in these chapters and why?

4 Show how the various mysteries are resolved in this section.

5 By close reference to what is said, explain M.Paul's behaviour. What evidence is there that he is really in love with Lucy?

Charlotte Brontë's art in *Villette*
The characters

Lucy Snowe

I am constitutionally nervous.

Lucy has a vivid imagination and is very sensitive. Since she is the narrator – in a sense it is her 'autobiography' we are reading – we register her reactions first and foremost in every situation which occurs. She is observant, as we see from the scenes at Bretton; very impressionable, as we see from her visit to London. She is independent, and possessed of much courage, as we see when she determines to try her fortune abroad and goes to Villette. But since her account spans the whole novel – it is her voice we hear all the time – this section will be very selective in order to avoid running into unreasonable lengths.

First of all Lucy, like her predecessor Jane Eyre, has a strong and abiding need to be loved. This is evident from her attachment to the Bretton home and her godmother in particular. Here she has a sense of belonging which is essential to her security. When Paulina arrives we are aware of the quality of Lucy's observation. In some ways she is critical of the child, and defensive about her own stance – 'I, Lucy Snowe, plead guiltless of that curse, an overheated and discursive imagination' (page 69). This may be so in her young days, but it is not true later, as there are many instances in the Rue Fossette of Lucy's imagination taking flight into nervous depression. As she watches Paulina we get the impression that she is living vicariously: indeed this is Lucy's lot for much of the narrative, as we see when she begins to take an interest, much later, in the grown-up Paulina and her developing relationship with Graham Bretton.

Lucy at Bretton is observer and narrator: withdrawn, she has to hear Graham say to his mother (of Paulina) 'she amuses me a great deal more than you or Lucy Snowe' (page 85). Although happy at Bretton, Lucy is very much the outsider as long as Paulina is there (Paulina comes to appreciate Lucy's real worth much later). Lucy however develops her interest in children, here through this particular one, an interest she is to turn to

good account when she goes to Villette. She has a natural sympathy for Paulina, however; comforts her before she goes,
warms her and holds her, knowing what the child is suffering
when she is about to leave Graham. This sympathetic trait is a
mark of Lucy's character: it is repeated later when M.Paul is not
present and Madame Beck announces his departure. Lucy puni-
shes a child, but afterwards alone, comforts her. Despite her
reserved nature, Lucy has the need to give love, to convey a
warmth which is repressed in her exterior and public behaviour.

Lucy as narrator is of course highly selective. The period
before she goes to Miss Marchmont is teasingly passed over, and
when she devotes herself to the crippled old lady she surveys
herself honestly in the mirror, finding that she is a 'wan spectacle. The blight, I believed, was chiefly external: I still felt life at
life's sources.' (page 96) This capacity for inner experience is
one of the keys to Lucy's character. Only once, in the terrible
breakdown during her loneliness in the Rue Fossette which
drives her into the confessional of Père Silas, do we find her
relinquishing her hold on 'life's sources'. Lucy has courage and
resilience. Although in some ways she is victim, she is primarily
and positively a survivor. Lucy attracts the confidences of others,
and I do not mean this in any predatory way. Miss Marchmont,
on the night before her death, asks her to 'Be my chaplain' (page
101). Freed from that responsibility, Lucy, as always, listens to
her inner voices. 'Leave this wilderness'(page 104) is the instruc-
tion she obeys, though she holds regular inward debates with
Reason, Emotion etc before forming a judgment or deciding on
a course of action. When she goes to London she reacts as a
normal and impressionable person might: she is elated by the
experience, and responds to the adventure. It requires a rare
courage to do what she has done – the first independent mark,
soon to be extended by the trip to Villette. In London she shows
the intelligent observation which is one of her main characteristics: 'At the West-end you may be amused, but in the city you are
deeply excited.' (page 109). She wins the respect of the waiter;
knows she is cheated by the porter; is soon aware of the snob-
beries on board the ship; and tolerates the chatter and selfishness of Ginevra Fanshawe despite her own 'nerves'. We are
aware of her intense loneliness and the fear which she conquers
when she stays at the inn for the night. Again she is prompted by
an inward voice, this one telling her to 'Go to Villette' (page 121)

She survives the trunk adventure, from which she is rescued by the unrecognized Graham Bretton, and then meets Madame Back and endures the scrutiny of M.Paul. As I said earlier – she survives – and the result is employment. It says much for Lucy's resilience that she also survives the visit of the spying Madame Beck in the dead of night.

Lucy soon makes her way. Thrown in at the deep end by being faced with a class, she shows character and exacts discipline by making an example of an exceptionable girl. This is the first battle that she wins, but it is the crucial one. Lucy is always capable of conquering her fear (with the one exception mentioned above) and indeed she secretly enjoys taking on difficulties. She studies hard, works hard, has a keen insight into the nature of her pupils and an even keener one into the character and practices of Madame Beck. As an English teacher in a Belgian school, as a Protestant (and Lucy is fiercely Protestant) in a Catholic centre, Lucy is still an outsider. Although she describes some of her lessons as being 'on the edge of a moral volcano' (page 146) she is intent on success and works at the means of achieving it. She studies the nature of the Labassecouriennes' mind, and practises accordingly. But she is aware too that her Protestant views are reported to Madame Beck.

Ginevra reappears in her life, and we get the impression that although Lucy despises her shallowness, she also envies her attractiveness. In this situation Lucy shows her character. She can put Ginevra down by blunt comments from time to time which the other accepts. This is a tribute to Lucy's force of character. Lucy is not above laughing at the seriousness with which Ginevra takes herself. Lucy now becomes observer of Dr John and, ever speculative, wonders if Madame Beck has ideas about marrying him. She also feels, quite erroneously, that Dr John is having an affair with Rosine. And this is something that we should remember about Lucy – frequently her judgments of character and situations, particularly the latter, are not always completely accurate. Charlotte Brontë is subtly presenting a character which is recognizable as a character in life, that is, fallible.

Lucy, though afraid of loneliness, likes to be solitary, and finds her most tranquil moments in the secluded garden. The fact that this avenue is shunned by the others again underlines

Lucy's independence and her courage. It moves her to reminiscence of her childhood but, not only that, it moves her towards a greater wish for self-expression and fulfilment, though it is doubtful whether she would articulate it as such. Because of the 'billet' she finds herself the confidante of Graham up to a point (he does not at this stage reveal the object of his attentions). She becomes irritated by Madame Beck's spying, but has sufficient humour to laugh at it. On the eve of the fête, Lucy spends some time waxing satirical about her fellow teachers. Then her life changes: M.Paul whirls into it and she finds herself taking part in the vaudeville. Even here she overcomes her fear and asserts her independence, refusing to wear some of the man's clothes on stage. Lucy however takes great delight in wooing Ginevra on stage and watching Dr John's reactions. Her puritanism comes to the fore though when she repents her delight in performance. To some extent her reaction makes her take it out on Ginevra, and she is now able to be satirical too about the diminutive de Hamal. Lucy is always capable of spirit, and she displays it here when she sneers at Ginevra for even comparing de Hamal to Dr John. This is an insight into Lucy's own feelings for Dr John, which are soon to be more positively apparent to her. Lucy responds to Dr John's telling her how much he loves Ginevra with a generosity of feeling. She even urges him to hope by saying that his own feelings will evoke some like response in Ginevra. It is kindly meant because she sees his suffering.

The nature of Lucy's susceptibility is shown in the long vacation (described in detail in Chapter 15 of Volume One). We have noted that she is much influenced by changes of weather, and after the heat here comes the rain. Part of Lucy's trouble is her active imagination, for she is able to picture what her companions are doing while she is left. With the storms Lucy becomes delirious although, when she ventures forth, it is a considered cry for help. There is the major irony that she is turning to the Catholicism that she hates, and this is an indication of the greatness of her need. As she puts it, 'I was perishing for a word of advice or an accent of comfort' (page 233), but such is her inner strength that, although she faints later, she sees into the motivation of the priest who has been kind to her. Rigidly anti-Catholic, Lucy fears the persuasions of conversion. Lucy in her weakness does not know where she is. She soon finds that she is with friends (though the plot creaks here with the fortuitous reappearance of Mrs Bretton and Graham, who is Dr John) and her gratitude turns to love. She waits for Dr John in the evenings, enjoying the consideration and solicitude that he always shows her. But Lucy responds with a typically fierce outburst when Dr John tells her how superior in the human virtues Ginevra is. He is right when he ascribes Lucy's outburst to jealousy, but only in part. Lucy knows Ginevra only too well, and cannot resist telling Dr John how misplaced his love for her is.

She causes herself much anguish by saying it, and her need for the reassurance and forgiveness from him is such that she apologizes. Happy is his forgiveness, she even keeps her sense of humour intact, being able to tease Dr John about Madame's devotion to him. Her appreciation of all that he does for her is high. Her condemnation of the 'Cleopatra', however, reveals another aspect of Lucy's character. This is her rejection of the full-blooded and voluptuous, something that is part of her puritanical make-up and also part of her feeling of physical inferiority. Lucy is conscious that she has little outward sex-appeal. She takes a genuine delight in the concert, though this does not stop her criticising the performers. Her critical faculty never seems to be in abeyance – it is always being exercised on those around her. She is quick to resent any slight to Graham and Mrs Bretton, hence her focus on Ginevra when that young lady is subjecting them to her satirical appraisal.

After all their kindness, there is little surprise when Lucy leaves the Brettons for us to find her upset at the return to the Pensionnat. Once more we have the inward dialogue about herself and her future. This characteristic is overtaken by the re-entry into her life of M.Paul in all his unpredictable and moody ebullience. He tries to get her to talk, but Lucy is so overcome at parting from her friends that she breaks down and cries. Lucy wants to be alone, and rejects the demanding advances of Ginevra too. She returns to what she calls expressively 'the palsy of custom' (page 317). She is lifted by a letter from Graham (though perhaps a little aware of M.Paul's jealousy) and made happier in her loneliness. And here we get more evidence of Lucy's 'nerves'. First, the apparition of the nun unhinges her, and, second, when they go to the room she is convinced that her letter has disappeared. Part of Lucy's nervous trouble is something like a persecution complex. To be fair, this is understandable when one thinks of Madame Beck's constant 'surveillance'.

Lucy, her feelings of love for Graham kept under strict control, is pleased that he has seen through Ginevra Fanshawe. Taking the cue from Graham, she says (page 334) 'A new creed became mine – a belief in happiness'. She is taken to the theatre, and, because of the fire, meets Paulina and her father (not yet identified). The theatre experience is as interesting as the picture-gallery, for Lucy is not slow to see theatre as 'a mighty revelation' on the one hand and as 'a spectacle low, horrible, immoral' (page 339) on the other. She is undermined – Lucy is always susceptible – by the fact that she doesn't get any letters from Dr John for six weeks. When she receives one from Mrs Bretton her happiness returns. Invited there, Lucy becomes observer again, the observer (not voyeur) of Graham and the grown-up (just) Paulina. She sees the way things are going. Lucy feels some happiness in her own friendship here though, for she greatly respects M.de Bassompierre and thinks of him as a true gentleman. Lucy is now moving easily and naturally in a society which has hitherto been closed to her. On the winter day that she stays at La Terrasse in their company, Lucy, ever-conscious of the weather, wishes to be quiet and is allowed to be so by the considerateness of 'The Little Countess'.

Lucy's reaction to the developing love between Graham and Paulina is to bury her letters in the old tree, a symbolic renunciation of her love for Graham and an acknowledgment of Madame's reading them. Another encounter with the nun finds her more stoically silent and infinitely less hysterical. She shares Paulina's criticism of Ginevra but, when she attends the lecture, we note the movement of her feelings towards M.Paul. She refers to 'his flame of purity' (page 397), sufficient indication of the esteem and warmth in which she holds him. She is hurt by Graham's light raillery with her, and surprised when M.Paul approaches them and is insulting. Lucy herself has to brave his wrath when she enters a class to give him a message. Here we feel that she is forcing herself to do this, and that the action perhaps takes the place of what she cannot put into words. She also puts her feelings into another action – the making of the watchguard for his 'fête'. But when she is reprimanded for her levity in dress she exposes M.Paul to the sarcasm which is her weapon of defence. She is angry within, since she is the last person who should have been accused of worldly vanity.

She is even more angry on the day, when M.Paul releases his frustrations at not receiving a present from her by an attack on the English which provokes a patriotic outburst from Lucy. We have to admit that Lucy does show, from time to time in her observations on Labassecouriennes, that she is insular in her attitudes. She is more than softened when she finds M.Paul at her desk, conscious that he has visited it before and placed volumes and magazines for her which have given her intellectual and emotional sustenance. Lucy becomes obsessed with him. He is now *her* teacher, stimulating her to greater depth discovery. She realizes that he sees in her a particular and exciting talent. Lucy's own ambitions are stirred when he provokes her or sneers at her. But she is also aware – and this is what Lucy needs – of his kindness. When he puts the shawls over her he is doing more, in a sense, than Graham Bretton did in writing letters to her. She returns to her renunciation of Dr John with some doubt, but her words by the tree are overheard by M.Paul, and this time he reveals more of himself to her. Despite her apprehensive 'I am constitutionally nervous' (page 456) he tells her of the affinity between them. She, puritanical and rightly so here, disapproves of his claim that he has spied on her and others. From this intensity Lucy finds herself drawn into the confidences of Paulina about Graham. She acts nobly in the interests of their happiness, but seems to be on the edge of losing her own. When M.Paul hints to her at the picnic that he might go away, Lucy finds that her face is covered with tears. She admits that she were rather he were brusque than tender. He has called her his sister, but that is not enough.

Lucy's trip to Madame Walravens is the eye-opener that Madame Beck and Père Silas have decreed, but it has a double action. Of course it gives her despair by making her think that M.Paul is beyond her reach, but it also makes her love all the stronger because of the fact that she now knows that M.Paul has a self-sacrificing nature, that he goes without on behalf of others. Lucy's moods on the visit are again complemented by the weather, here a terrible storm. She wants to be with M.Paul all the more, but first she has to endure humiliation at the hands of the professors who examine her. With typical independent spirit she takes them on in her essay, and then proceeds to question M.Paul about his own existence. After some time, she tells him (she is made secure by his expressions of amity) that she feels the mystery of the nun and the attendant mysteries will be explained. Lucy by now is beginning to register the deeper changes in M.Paul. She reacts when he only nods to her, and soon comes to realize that he is making an attempt to convert her through the influence of Père Silas. She also learns how to cope with this, and with an accretion of humour mocks the questions M.Paul asks her about the effect the tract had on her. She further resists the attempts to convert her through the display of ceremonial. But she again receives reassurance of his love when he says to her 'God guide us all! God bless you, Lucy!' (page 517). It is the generous expression of faith and love which goes beyond dogma.

Again Lucy turns aside from her own affairs in the cause of Paulina and Graham. It is not so much that she is positive as discreet, diplomatic. Her handling of M.de Bassompierre is evidence of this. Moreover, before his interview Graham is sustained by Lucy's faith and genuine kindness. When all is well, we realize the depth and sincerity of Lucy's feelings for the young couple. There follows for Lucy the full effects of shock. The news of M.Paul's leaving finds Lucy suffering the pangs of frustration, bewilderment, apprehension. She looks back on her happiness of ten days earlier with him, but remembers the confrontation with Madame Beck and Père Silas, and wonders if this explains the sudden decision. M.Paul's letter with its injunction to wait is a great comfort to her. Then she suspects Madame Beck of having marital designs on M.Paul; stays up at night waiting for him in vain, and then comes to the next evening which 'found me like the first – untamed, tortured, again pacing a solitary room in an unalterable passion of silent desolation' (page 546). The words are an eloquent definition of Lucy's distraught state.

Lucy's escape through the paling and her watching her friends at the night fête in the park is exciting narrative. Despite her state, she takes great delight in seeing all the bustling activity. She also likes following her 'friends viewlessly' (page 550). She appreciates the courteous attentions of Monsieur Liret. She is touched when she hears herself spoken of benevolently by Graham and his mother, but even here there is some mention of her reserve and the fact that she is 'little moved' (page 554).If they only knew the truth about Lucy's febrile inner nature. But her anger and spirit are roused by 'the secret junta' (page 558). She discovers Madame Beck's lie (M.Paul had not sailed as she said he would). But when she returns to the pensionnat she has to endure the sight of the ghostly nun, fortunately for the last time.

Lucy has two fine moments in the final sequence of the novel. The first is when M.Paul stands up to Madame Beck — 'He was roused, and I loved him in his wrath with a passion beyond what I had yet felt.' (page 581). The second is when she sees what he has done for her. Her love is enhanced by her capacity to endure, and the three years separation, involving work, devotion, fulfilment of ambition, all these are expressive of her love for M.Paul. Whether he does return, or whether he perishes in the storms, is almost irrelevant. His letters represent him, and Lucy has what she most wants: to be loved. There are times when Lucy's narrowness, her particular obsessions, bias, neuroses may irritate us. But we are never less than with her, caught up in her narrative experience and living her suffering. Lucy is a triumph of full characterization.

Graham Bretton

his waved light auburn hair, his supple symmetry, his smile frequent, and destitute neither of fascination nor of subtlety . . .

This quotation gives Graham's initial attractiveness, something to which the small Paulina and the adult Lucy (and Paulina) respond. At first he adopts a teazing attitude towards the little girl (we must remember that he is only sixteen himself at the time). His picking her up, apart from the verbal raillery, shows a degree of condescension and, it must be allowed, insensitivity. He also acts up, sulking apparently in order to draw Polly's (Paulina's) attention to him. He does allow her to manage him a little, but his egoistic absorption with his friends shows the thoughtless side of his nature. When Lucy overhears him say that Paulina affords him more amusement than she and his mother do, we realize that the young Graham, for all his attractiveness, is shallow.

Graham helps Lucy when she arrives in Villette, though initially he seems to be weighing up the possibilities of so doing. Lucy feels that 'He was a true young English gentleman.' (page 125). It is in Chapter 10 (Dr John) that we first see the adult

Graham (not recognized as that yet) in action. His treatment of Fifine displays his professional competence and judgment, a certain natural kindness. He impresses Madame, but Lucy notes that perhaps his eyes pass too quickly from face to face. She also feels that he is capable of laughing at what is going on, as indeed he demonstrates later. He is firm and genial and the children too are attracted to him. He is amenable, and goes along with what Madame wants. He is punctual, but gives Madame 'rallying looks' (page 162). He is observant: he notices that Lucy is studying him attentively (of course because she has the idea that she knows who he may be).

Dr John's kindness to Lucy is repeated at greater length after her visit to Père Silas. But his weakness, his essential susceptibility, is shown with regard to Ginevra. He is in a comfortable position in relation to Madame Beck – he is mischievous about any designs she may have on him – but Lucy becomes his confidant with regard to the worthless Ginevra. He obviously bribes Rosine, is mindful of Ginevra's attachment to de Hamal, and is intolerant of that diminutive man. So anxious is he to succeed with Ginevra that he is for some time blind to her faults. It is when she satirically surveys his mother at the theatre that he sees into her. Thereafter her fascination wanes. He binds Lucy to silence about Ginevra's earlier indiscretion, but talks much more freely to her after the theatre incident. Before that we note one thing – that although he is kind to Lucy he seems oblivious of her feelings for him. If he is aware, he treats her as if he is flattered, but no more than that.

When Lucy stays with Graham and his mother at La Terrasse, he shows that he is singularly blind in not recognizing her. Lucy however is soon feeling deeply for him – he is 'Strong and cheerful, and firm and courteous; not rash, yet valiant' (page 250). He also diagnoses Lucy correctly, noting her nervous disposition, and he certainly does his best to relieve her pressures by taking her out – theatre, concert and visits to art galleries. He forgives Lucy her condemnation of Ginevra. He also reveals that he still has his youthful capacity to tease.

Dr John is adept at taking responsibility, whether it be for a coach when the driver is tipsy, or medical and practical action, as when the fire occurs. Notice how his 'quick eyes' spot Lucy's letter on the floor, and how he calms her hysteria on that evening of the apparition so calmly and directly. He exerts authority with ease, and is used to being obeyed. He fades from the action, except in relation to Lucy's observation of his courtship of Paulina. Graham is very taken with Paulina, but this subdues him in her company at times. He picks up his teasing attitude again when he involves Lucy in discussion about Ginevra, though it is obvious he is only doing this in order to have her compared, disadvantageously, with Paulina. He has some vanity, remembering when prompted by Lucy how much Paulina preferred him at Bretton. When M.Paul attacks Lucy Graham enjoys what is for him a joke. But his approach to M.de Bassompierre is respectful and cautious: Lucy knows that Graham has to have status, but she allows 'All that was best in Graham sought Paulina' (page 518). When she has cheered him before he sees M.de Bassompierre she knows he will succeed 'He was born victor, as some are born vanquished.' (page 529). He wins Paulina, though she does most of the talking to her father.

M.Paul Emanuel

a small, dark and spare man, in spectacles.

This is our first sight of M.Paul, and Lucy's too. He is an arresting character mainly because of his paradoxical nature. He is officious, proud, zealous, inexorable, mercurial, quick-tempered, passionate, and in Lucy's interactions with him he is all those things and more. Lucy has evidence also of his tenderness, and smarts under his vituperation. He is a dictator, but, and this is where our credulity is stretched, he also has a heart of gold: serving Madame Beck; prepared to go to Guadaloupe on behalf of Madame Walravens and the 'junta'; devoted to the memory of the young girl; and also treasuring his god-daughter and seeing that she is in a position to marry. If he is fire, he is also intellect: his fury when interrupted is more than balanced by his ability to deliver a lecture which learned men respect. He is a talented theatrical producer, but the kind of man too who takes his pupils out on a picnic and manages all the preparations. He is bossy, solitary, loved by his spaniel and by Lucy, loved and feared by his pupils, an autocrat but a brilliant and inspiring man. If he is based on M.Héger, then M.Héger must have been remarkable. He is secretive, planning Lucy's future as schoolmistress: he is devoted to his religion, and therefore he and Père Silas must plan the conversion of Lucy, which is not successful. In short, he is a man for all seasons, spilling into caricature which, despite his physique, is larger even than eccentric life. He has vivacity but without the substance of being. The result is curious. There are times when M.Paul is like a puppet, other times when he is like a man. There are some marvellous strokes, as when he unobtrusively puts the shawls over Lucy, which almost bring him alive. There are other sequences when he is way outside credibility. Take, for example, his accosting Lucy to abuse her when she is looking at the Cleopatra, or take his fantastic presentation of her before the two professors in order to demonstrate that his marking and judgment of her have been right as distinct from theirs. It is always difficult to accept anyone who is clearly petty black and tender white. In a novel which has many realistic sequences M.Paul strikes one as the stuff of romance. Perhaps it is that he caused Charlotte Brontë trouble too. It would be difficult to see him living with Lucy, for the dynamics of his character were hardly made for domesticity. He is a remarkable creation, but lacking the integration of psychological realism.

Madame Beck

I felt she was not one to be led an inch by her feelings: grave and considerate, she gazed, consulting her judgment ...

Madame Beck, despite her dumpy figure, is a formidable person. She is successful because she can deal with any situation, except in her final scene with Lucy and M.Paul, where the latter is too much for her. She depends on 'surveillance', and her power is based on that. She reads Lucy's letters, encourages her minions to spy and report back to her, thus ensuring that she knows all that goes on in her school and that she will be able therefore to forestall or dismiss at will. She does depend to some extent on M.Paul, getting him to approve Lucy before she takes her on. She also has a soft spot for Dr John, indulges it, seems to be encouraging him, and certainly checks up on his relationship with Lucy. Because of his humour she does not go too far – we doubt whether she would anyway – but she shows herself to be a brilliant diplomat, talking the parents into acceptance of this new young medical practitioner who does not belong to their faith. Madame Beck's performance is masterly and has both ridiculous and triumphant moments. For example her 'sneeze out of season' shows that she has been listening to the conversation between Lucy and Dr John. Her handling of the eager young males at the fête dance is masterly again in its authority.

Yet we find it hard to believe that she should command respect. She is an evil woman intent on maintaining power by manipulation. Consider her sending Lucy to Madame Walravens. On the one hand she is hoping to propitiate the old woman, on the other hoping to persuade Lucy of the hopelessness of her position with M.Paul. Lucy in her heightened reactions feels that Madame wants to marry M.Paul, that she is predatory and dangerous, and that M.Paul himself is under her thumb. She is strangely indulgent over her children, avoids confrontation as much as she can, but is capable of being unperturbed for the most part. She is feline and devious, capable of blackmail and anger, though the latter is largely repressed by her natural exercise of power. She is a positively malign character, Lucy's cynical appraisal of her bigotry matched by her unequivocal condemnation of what Madame Beck represents in education.

Ginevra Fanshawe

she tormented me with an unsparing selfishness

Lucy meets Ginevra on the boat across to the port of Boue-Marine. She is talkative, silly, vain, shallow, superficial, in fact the very antithesis of Lucy. She is also a snob who sets great store by money and position, and she is naturally flirtatious. She absorbs Lucy's atention on this trip, but she also provides useful information by telling her of Madame Beck's school. She looks down on Lucy, but enjoys the situation of being apparently able to boss her about — I say apparently because Lucy soon reveals that she knows how best to deal with Ginevra's type. Ginevra has no strength under adversity, and part of her motivation is to avoid work and poverty (her father is an officer on half-pay, and she fears economic dependence).

At Madame Beck's Ginevra is 'a thriving pupil' (page 148). She constantly buttonholes Lucy in order to talk almost non-stop about her romantic attachments — the little de Hamal and the large Dr John. She has an entry into society in Villette through Mrs Cholmondeley, and lets Lucy know it. Her conversation, when it is not about the two men, is superficial and repetitious.

She also indulges her expensive tastes, and some of her presents come from de Hamal. Lucy is aware of the moral culpability of this. She tries to get Ginevra to return the gifts, but Ginevra goes away laughing, happy in her irresponsibility. Ginevra plays in the vaudeville opposite Lucy. It is type-casting, since she is a coquette both on and off the stage.

She opens the ball which follows the play – 'she was the child of pleasure' (page 211). She is exhilarated by the experience of opening the ball and being what Lucy calls the belle of it. But she comes down to earth moodily, and, as always, seeks Lucy out for her confidences. She plays off Isadore and Alfred against each other, but conveys her snobbery and shame over Isadore. Lucy puts her down when she is in this kind of mood. She shows time and time again that she can handle the small vanities of Ginevra.

Ginevra makes her big mistake in being satirically observant of Dr John and his mother. She is already intriguing with de Hamal, and the whole of the nun-apparition part of the novel derives from his disguise in his clandestine meetings with Ginevra. The latter obviously encourages him, and this is the cause of Dr John's basic concern about her when he asks Lucy to watch over her. Her letter to Lucy announcing her elopement and revealing the details of what she and de Hamal have done is typical of her nature. She has enjoyed the deception, exulting in the way she has used people, got her portion and her social position. Yet her letters relating details of her son's ailments show that she needs to keep in touch with Lucy. Despite the debts of her marriage, Ginevra survives, calling for sympathy and getting it, always victim of her own selfishness. She is a study in shallow egoism.

Mrs Bretton

Mrs Bretton was not generally a caressing woman: even with her deeply-cherished son, her manner was rarely sentimental . . .

Mrs Bretton is good-hearted, doting on Graham in his child-hood and his adulthood. She is not fully developed as a charac-ter through Lucy's eyes, but we remember her concern for Paulina, her protecting the child against too much teasing, her care and concern for Lucy too. She disappears from the action for long periods, but we note that when Lucy is at La Terrasse, Mrs Bretton, despite the passage of some ten years, has not changed. She is kind, thoughtful, proud of her son (sometimes their exchanges are a little cloying) and very anxious to see Lucy restored to health. She is still sharp, recognizing Lucy before Graham does. She is naturally pleased by Graham's courtship of Paulina in adulthood, though she plays but little part in it. She has none of the possessive tendencies of M.de Bassompierre.

Paulina Mary

The young Paulina seen through Lucy's eyes is a curious mixture of precocity (of manner), pathos, whimsical behaviour and attempted independence. She is initially independent of Lucy too, but she is reduced by her imminent parting from Graham to turn to Lucy for comfort, and to use her as a messenger. The heartbreak of the child is moving, and when we meet her all those years later we find that she shows many of the same characteristics that she showed earlier. But the oppressions of the little woman have become subdued into happier tints in the grown one. She is devoted to her father as she had been as a child (again the possessiveness of the relationship is somewhat cloying to the reader) and she soon becomes aware that her feelings for Graham have deepened with the years. There is nothing more touching in *Villette* than her confiding in Lucy, her revealing her love for Graham, and the exquisite sensitivity that she shows in thinking of her father and helping to resolve the situation by the quality of her own sensitivity.

M.de Bassompierre

M.de Bassompierre exists on the caricature level of possessive father, pathetic in Paulina's youth, selfish and not a little arrogant in her maturity. The trouble is that he has not allowed himself to think of her as grown up, and feels sorry for himself when he feels that he is to lose her. He is a demanding man, and has a consciousness of rank which makes him, albeit temporarily, look down on Graham as a suitor for his daughter's hand. Although Lucy can speak of him as the perfect gentleman, and although he shows breeding and discretion with regard to her subordinate position as a teacher in a school, he does not arouse the reader's sympathy.

Other characters

The other characters come alive fitfully. *Zélie de St. Pierre*, is an example, with her malicious tongue and her flirtatious attitude towards M. Paul. She also has an excessive consciousness of status. The Beck children *Désirée* and *Fifine* register in passing. *Madame Walravens* is a deliberate caricature grotesque, and *Père Silas* something of a caricature priest too, intent on converting the temporarily vulnerable Lucy. There *is* an unevenness in the characterization of *Villette*, yet here too there is an indication of subtlety. Lucy is the seeing narrator, but what is suggested is that because of her own feelings and obsessions, she sees the superficial in some people and a greater depth in others. That, I suggest, is a faithful record of what we all see in life, and it contributes to our aesthetic and vital appreciation of the novel.

Style

The basic technique employed by Charlotte Brontë in *Villette* is that of first-person narrative: as with *Jane Eyre*, we feel that we are reading autobiography, but we must always remember that it is *fictional* autobiography. Although Lucy may exhibit many of the facets of what we take to be Charlotte's character, we must not confuse the author with literary creation. The early narrative, that is, the Bretton sections right through to the arrival in *Villette*, is admirably clear. It is direct, simple, engaging. Take the first sentence of the novel, for example: 'My godmother lived in a handsome house in the clean and ancient town of Bretton' (page 61). It is this kind of simplicity which distinguishes the early Lucy – a rather different person in terms of fears, apprehensions, love – from the later Lucy, beset by situations and pressures. The style in the early chapters seems to be conditoned by the fact that Lucy, here as at other points in the narrative, is an observer who is recording events with lucid emphasis for the reader. The *dialogue* which she registers, and this quality runs throughout the novel, is natural and unforced. The only time that it verges on the unusual and eccentric is in the utterances of M.Paul. But these are in themselves reflective of his character – he is individualistically different in his own right, and the language used of him and by him is necessarily so too.

The mastery of dialogue is seen particularly in the Bretton sequence, with Paulina's words again indicative of her curious mixture of precocity, uncertainty, pathos. But there is an inner mastery too as the feelings of Lucy are exposed by her to us, the readers. This balance is indeed maintained throughout the novel. Thus when there has been considerable verbal teasing between Graham and Paulina, the latter has to say goodbye to her father. He adopts a third person tone towards her ('Then Polly must be cheerful' page 79) which is natural in view of her age and the circumstances. This is complemented by the observer of the scene, Lucy, saying to the reader 'I, Lucy Snowe, was calm' (page 79). This dual effect, of Lucy observing and reacting, is central to the narrative tensions of *Villette*.

When Lucy settles in the pensionnat she is, in more senses than one, in a foreign land. I refer to her spiritual and linquistic differences as well as the actual physical location. The fact that she is an outsider is given a considerable stress by the use of French dialogue which is natural in the case of Madame Beck, M.Paul and Zélie de St Pierre, for example. But French is also used to indicate the fact that Lucy is adaptable and fluent; and that she is gradually becoming integrated into the situation in the pensionnat. It is significant that when M.Paul manages to insult Great Britain Lucy's patriotic fervour is kindled in an outbrust in *French*. She is ensuring that although she had adopted the language she rejects the views associated with it here in M.Paul's denunciation.

Part of Charlotte Brontë's style in *Villette* is devoted to the creation of *atmosphere*. This is cleverly varied. Consider, for example, the Bretton atmosphere, the atmosphere on the night of Miss Marchmont's death, or the lonely Lucy in London, or her reactions and adjustments on board the boat which takes her to Boue-Marine. Most impressive for the reader are the atmospheres of the Rue Fossette: Madame Beck or M.Paul in Lucy's dormitory, the atmosphere of deception, secrecy, what is called 'surveillance'; the atmosphere in class, particularly during Lucy's first lesson, where she triumphs fortuitously but comes dangerously close to failure. A Gothic atmosphere is engendered whenever the 'nun' appears: Lucy's garden retreat has its own tranquillity, which is disturbed by strange actions and the fears of spying. There is the claustrophobic atmosphere of the confessional and Père Silas; the grotesque and equally claustrophobic feeling about the abode of Madame Walravens; and a fine sense of the panoramic and public in the visit to the theatre, M.Paul's lecture and even the 'vaudeville' of the pensionnat. But again the duality is present, for the most intense atmosphere of all is that which conveys Lucy's feelings, sufferings, loneliness and illness at the height of her depression in the Long Vacation. This inner atmosphere – the fever of the consciousness – is very important to our understanding of *Villette*. We see everything through the eyes and the reactions of the heroine. The best example of the atmospheric evocation is found in the superb sequence where

Lucy, instead of succumbing to the drug, gets up and goes to the park at night seeing, in heightened and almost kaleido-scopic effect, all those characters who have impinged with various degrees of intensity on her life. It is hard to define the atmosphere, except to say that it is brilliantly charged with clarity of a visionary nature. Once more Lucy is observer, but her heart is completely involved. Her movement home and the discovery of the effigy of the nun on her bed shows how quickly and effectively Charlotte Brontë changes the mood.

Although the Gothic elements in *Villette* have been criticized adversely, we should remember always that we are being invited to share the experiences of a neurotic and intense young woman. It is one of Charlotte Brontë's major achieve-ments that her style is always consonant with the experiences of Lucy Snowe. Lucy has a range of reference herself. She is religious, and there are a number of Biblical allusions, as we have seen from the chapter commentaries. These two fit the nature of the subject, for Lucy is on a kind of pilgrimage in which she not only finds love but also finds herself. There is a range of literary reference, some serious and weighty, some ironic, like the running references to *The Arabian Nights*. Lucy's own reportage is sometimes balanced even antithetical ('a doubtful state between patronage and politeness' (page 107). There are also a number of vivid and sudden metaphors and similes, for example Lucy speaks of such things as 'my spirit shook its always-fettering wings half loose', then adds in the same paragraph that 'my soul grew as fast as Jonah's gourd', and explaining her sudden wish to travel as an escape from 'the eating rust of obscurity'. (page 108). All these are emblematic of her and of an almost colourfully casual style.

Apart from the figurative layers, there are also the twists and turns of self-communication and communion as Lucy looks into herself. The narrative 'I' is a frequent emphasis. There are addresses to the reader ('Reader, I felt alarmed!' page 241) which establish the intimacy of the confidences being offered. There are digressions, but these are few and far between. The texture of the writing is remarkable for its clarity and the ability to create strong visual effects in a few strokes. Take the scene in the art gallery where Lucy contemplates the Cleopatra (Chapter 19). In her comments and observations on the portrait Lucy uses an immediacy of language which corresponds to the immediate impact of the pictures. In other words, style fits content and vice-versa. There is no page in *Villette* where we are not drawn to the independent force of the writing in its direct exposure of experience.

Setting

There are three settings in *Villette*, though only the locations in Villette (Brussels) are of major importance. The first of these is Bretton, an old town in Yorkshire which seems to be derived from Bridlington as well as York and Leeds. The next is London, with mention of The Cornhill, Paternoster Row, the Strand, Temple Gardens and the West End on Lucy's fleeting visit. When she leaves London she goes to Boue-Marine, a French port which is not clearly identifiable. Villette is the capital of Labassecour, Charlotte's name for Belgium, the Basse-Ville being the lower part of the capital. Haute-Ville is virtually the opposite, the park area of Brussels much frequented by the fashionable. There would be little point in tracing all the identifications from the Rue Fossette to La Terrasse. Suffice to say that the name and nature of the city is given in large by Lucy's journeys, whether they be to the park, to Madame Walravens or to the theatre: there is an authentic stamp about it all. The biographical tracings of Charlotte's stay in Brussels have been given in the section on The author and her work. The interior settings are as convincing as the exterior ones. In this novel the sense of place is pre-eminent, for in each case Lucy's experiences are intimately connected with the location in which she finds herself. The same is true of us all in life, and this is what establishes the major strand of realism in *Villette*.

Themes

The major theme of the novel is the struggle for *independence*. This struggle is also a prominent feature of Charlotte's own writing life. Lucy is an orphan, she is dependent on others, but after the death of Miss Marchmont she strikes out on her own. This theme of independence is linked obviously to that of *courage*. Even in just making up her mind to go to London Lucy is showing her bravery, her determination to face the world and make something for herself in it. True she becomes dependent on Madame Beck, first for the post of governess to her children, then as a teacher in her school. But we note throughout this Lucy's independence, her existence, although it means loneliness, in her own right. Indeed she so establishes this that Madame Beck will not get rid of her, such is her self-contained competence which, of course, is good for the school. The theme is curiously developed in the case of M.Paul. He shows commendable independence in attaching himself to Lucy despite the spiritual blackmail of Madame Beck and Père Silas; yet he hasn't enough independence to forsake them for Lucy at once.

Another theme which Lucy shares with M.Paul and indeed with Dr John is that of *responsibility*. Lucy is always responsible, seen in her concern for Paulina as a child (and an adult), her responsibility towards her pupils, her dedication to the school despite her reservations about its religious bias and the 'surveillance' of Madame Beck. Her own sense of responsibility is such that she takes a part in the play, learns it thoroughly, but with typical independence refuses to dress it fully. M.Paul's responsibility is there at every turn in his relation to the school and anything connected with it, and also to Madame Beck, Madame Walravens and his god-daughter. Dr John exemplifies responsibility to his patients, while both he and his mother show it towards Lucy after she has collapsed.

The theme of *love* runs throughout, with Paulina loving her father and Dr John, Lucy first loving Dr John and then M.Paul, and the latter finally confessing his love for Lucy. Lucy's need for love is a major stress: on a relatively comic level, we also feel Madame Beck's need.

The theme of *religious faith* or *duty* shows the divisions between Lucy and those around her in Villette. Lucy is religious, but has no use for fanaticism, and is particularly bitter in her resentment of the Catholic faith. She shows her objections when she is questioned by the girls in the school; she deplores the attempt to gain her as a convert by Père Silas, she resists the pamphlets and the arguments of M.Paul.

Another theme, implicit in the character of Madame Beck, is that of *power*, something to which M.Paul subscribes in his own eccentric way too. *Deception* runs throughout, with Madame's spying and M.Paul's attentions to Lucy's desk matched on another level by the sequence involving the 'nun' and Ginevra. With the latter there is the expression of *snobbery*, with M.de Bassompierre of *possessiveness* over his Polly. Mrs Bretton represents *kindness* and *integrity*, as does her son. *Selfishness* is rampant in Ginevra, Madame Beck, Madame Walravens and a minor character like Zélie de St Pierre. The themes of *Villette* derive from character and what it represents. In commentary and situation we are always aware of the moral adhesive.

General questions

1 What impression have you formed of Lucy Snowe during her stay in Villette?

Guideline notes

Introduction: how she came to be there — meeting with stranger (later recognized as Dr John) — engagement by Madame — meeting with M.Paul — baptism as teacher.

Courage in going — adjustment to situation (adaptability) — nervousness — awareness of nature of school and Madame — solitariness — reading — thinking — walks — own religious nature.

Need to be loved (advent of Dr John) — sense of responsibility — awareness of difference in religion — attitude (rather narrow-minded) towards Ginevra (and towards colleagues). Spirit (plays in vaudeville) — and of course independence — awareness of M.Paul.

The long vacation — developing illness — mental as well as physical — rambling — intense emotional need — confessional with Père Silas — mental collapse (and emotional) — awakening at La Terrasse — weakness — appreciation — beginnings of love for Dr John.

Attitude towards Dr John re Ginevra — kindness of Dr John — Lucy's dependence on him (the letters) — her reaction to the nun — her movement towards M.Paul — her reactions here — visit to Madame Walravens — its effects — various feelings for M.Paul (detail of at least three incidents).

Conclusion — nervous — sensitive — religious — but biassed against Catholics — need for love — courage — independence — integrity — moral responsibility — helping others (Paulina) — serious — largely solitary.

2 Compare and contrast Dr John and M.Paul.

3 Write an essay on the nature and practices of Madame Beck, referring closely to the text in your answer.

4 What do you find (a) humorous and (b) pathetic in the scenes at Bretton?

5 In what ways does Paulina the child anticipate in character the Paulina of young womanhood?

6 Compare Paulina as a young woman with Ginevra Fanshawe.

7 By close reference to the text, describe any *three* journeys undertaken by Lucy, indicating the particular effects and results that she experienced.

8 Say what effects the 'Gothic' incidents in the novel have upon our appreciation of it as a whole.

9 Write an essay in appreciation of the main elements of Charlotte Bronte's style in *Villette*.

10 Write a detailed account of any public scene in the novel which you enjoyed, bringing out clearly the nature of the atmosphere.

11 Do you find the dialogue in *Villette* convincing? You should refer both to the English and the French exchanges in your answer.

12 Which do you think is the most important theme in *Villette* and why? Quote from the text in your answer.

13 What aspect of the plot do you find most interesting? Again, quote from the text in your answer.

14 Compare and contrast any of the interiors in the book (i.e. that of La Terrasse with any part of the pensionnat).

15 Write an essay on any aspect of *Villette* not mentioned in the above questions.

Further reading

Other novels by Charlotte Brontë, particularly:
Jane Eyre
Shirley

Biography

Mrs Gaskell: *The Life of Charlotte Brontë* (1857: Penguin Edition 1975)
Winifred Gérin: *Charlotte Brontë: The Evolution of Genius* (Oxford 1967)

Criticism

Wendy Craik: *The Brontë Novels* (1968)
R. B. Martin: *Accents of Persuasion: Charlotte Brontë's Novels* (Faber 1966)

Companion

Everyman's Companion to the Brontës ed. Barbara and Gareth Lloyd Evans
(Dent 1982)

Pan study aids Titles published in the Brodie's Notes series

Edward Albee Who's Afraid of Virginia Woolf?

W. H. Auden Selected Poetry

Jane Austen Emma Mansfield Park Northanger Abbey Persuasion
Pride and Prejudice

Anthologies of Poetry Ten Twentieth Century Poets The Poet's Tale
The Metaphysical Poets

Samuel Beckett Waiting for Godot

Arnold Bennett The Old Wives' Tale

William Blake Songs of Innocence and Experience

Robert Bolt A Man for All Seasons

Harold Brighouse Hobson's Choice

Charlotte Brontë Jane Eyre Villette

Emily Brontë Wuthering Heights

Bruce Chatwin On the Black Hill

Geoffrey Chaucer (parallel texts editions) The Franklin's Tale
The Knight's Tale The Miller's Tale The Nun's Priest's Tale
The Pardoner's Tale Prologue to the Canterbury Tales
The Wife of Bath's Tale

John Clare Selected Poetry and Prose

Gerald Cole Gregory's Girl

Wilkie Collins The Woman in White

Joseph Conrad Heart of Darkness The Nigger of the Narcissus
Youth

Daniel Defoe Journal of a Plague Year

Shelagh Delaney A Taste of Honey

Charles Dickens David Copperfield Dombey and Son
Great Expectations Hard Times Little Dorrit Oliver Twist
Our Mutual Friend

Gerald Durrell My Family and Other Animals

George Eliot Middlemarch The Mill on the Floss Silas Marner

T. S. Eliot Murder in the Cathedral Selected Poems

J. G. Farrell The Siege of Krishnapur

W. Faulkner As I lay Dying

Henry Fielding Joseph Andrews Tom Jones

F. Scott Fitzgerald The Great Gatsby

E. M. Forster Howards End A Passage to India

E. Gaskell North and South

William Golding Lord of the Flies Rites of Passage The Spire

Oliver Goldsmith Two Plays of Goldsmith: She Stoops to Conquer;
The Good Natured Man

Graham Greene Brighton Rock The Human Factor
The Power and the Glory The Quiet American

Willis Hall The Long and the Short and the Tall

Thomas Hardy Chosen Poems of Thomas Hardy
Far from the Madding Crowd The Mayor of Casterbridge
Return of the Native Tess of the d'Urbervilles The Trumpet-Major
The Woodlanders

L. P. Hartley The Go-Between The Shrimp and the Anemone

Joseph Heller Catch-22

Ernest Hemingway A Farewell to Arms

Susan Hill I'm the King of the Castle

Barry Hines Kes

Aldous Huxley Brave New World

Henry James Washington Square

Ben Jonson Volpone

James Joyce A Portrait of the Artist as a Young Man Dubliners

John Keats Selected Poems and Letters of John Keats

D. H. Lawrence The Rainbow Sons and Lovers

Harper Lee To Kill a Mockingbird

Laurie Lee Cider with Rosie

Thomas Mann Death in Venice & Tonio Kröger

Christopher Marlowe Doctor Faustus Edward the Second

W. Somerset Maugham Of Human Bondage

Gavin Maxwell Ring of Bright Water

Thomas Middleton The Changeling

Arthur Miller The Crucible Death of a Salesman

John Milton A Choice of Milton's Verse Comus and Samson
Agonistes Paradise Lost I, II

Bill Naughton Spring and Port Wine

R. O'Brien Z for Zachariah

Sean O'Casey Juno and the Paycock
The Shadow of a Gunman and the Plough and the Stars

George Orwell Animal Farm 1984

John Osborne Luther

Alexander Pope Selected Poetry

J. B. Priestley An Inspector Calls

J. D. Salinger The Catcher in the Rye

Siegfried Sassoon Memoirs of a Fox-Hunting Man

Peter Shaffer The Royal Hunt of the Sun

William Shakespeare Antony and Cleopatra As You Like It
Coriolanus Hamlet Henry IV (Part I) Henry IV (Part II) Henry V
Julius Caesar King Lear Love's Labour's Lost Macbeth Measure for
Measure The Merchant of Venice A Midsummer Night's Dream
Much Ado about Nothing Othello Richard II Richard III Romeo and
Juliet The Sonnets The Taming of the Shrew The Tempest Twelfth
Night The Winter's Tale

G. B. Shaw Pygmalion Saint Joan

Richard Sheridan Plays of Sheridan: The Rivals; The Critic;
The School for Scandal

John Steinbeck The Grapes of Wrath Of Mice and Men The Pearl

Tom Stoppard Rosencrantz and Guildenstern are Dead

J. M. Synge The Playboy of the Western World

Jonathan Swift Gulliver's Travels

Dylan Thomas Under Milk Wood

Flora Thompson Lark Rise to Candleford

Anthony Trollope Barchester Towers

Mark Twain Huckleberry Finn

Keith Waterhouse Billy Liar

John Webster The Duchess of Malfi The White Devil

H. G. Wells The History of Mr Polly The War of the Worlds

Oscar Wilde The Importance of Being Earnest

William Wordsworth The Prelude (Books 1, 2)

William Wycherley The Country Wife

W. B. Yeats Selected Poetry

GCSE English coursework: Prose G. Handley and P. Wilkins

GCSE English coursework: Drama and Poetry: K. Dowling

PAN STUDY AIDS – ADVANCED

▶ The complete guide to exam success AT A level, Scottish Higher and Irish Higher School Certificate

▶ Authors are highly experienced teachers, examiners and textbook writers

▶ Covers all the essential points of every major exam syllabus, focusing on the areas which carry the most marks and paying particular attention to common points of difficulty

▶ Gives expert guidance on how to revise and prepare for the exams

▶ Illustrates the different types of exam questions, explaining what examiners look for

▶ Includes questions from past papers for practice.

Books in the series:

PAN STUDY AIDS – GCSE

▶ The complete guide to GCSE exam success

▶ Authors, highly experienced teachers, examiners and writers in every case, have taken account of ALL syllabuses in their subjects

▶ GCSE Study Aids cover all the essentials, focusing on the areas which carry the most marks and paying particular attention to common points of difficulty

▶ GCSE Study Aids supply expert guidance on how to revise and prepare for the exams

▶ GCSE Study Aids illustrate the varied types of exam questions, explaining exactly what examiners look for

▶ GCSE Study Aids give students the chance to practise their answers using sample questions supplied by the examination boards.

Books in the series: